EVERYDAY CONSUMER ENGLISH

Howard H. Kleinmann
Queens College,
City University of New York

Julie Weissman
Triton College
River Grove, Illinois

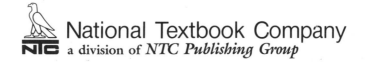
National Textbook Company
a division of NTC Publishing Group

97. 1285

Acknowledgment

This book was developed in part by the Allegheny Intermediate Unit, Pittsburgh, PA, as Project FACE, Howard H. Kleinmann, Project Director, Julie Weissman, Curriculum Specialist, with a grant from the Office of Consumers' Education, U.S. Office of Education, Department of Health, Education and Welfare.

Contents

$ Unit One **Budgets**

Unit Two **Banking—Savings Accounts**

Unit Three **Banking—Checking Accounts**

Unit Four **Supermarkets**

Unit Five **Supermarket Shopping**

Unit Six **Looking for an Apartment**

Unit Seven **Renting an Apartment**

Unit Eight **Buying Furniture and Appliances**

Preface

Everyday Consumer English is designed for individuals who want to improve their English-language skills while developing selected consumer life-skills. The premise of the book is that in order to be able to function effectively in American society, students of English must be able to apply their developing language skills in meaningful contexts, in situations they are likely to encounter every day.

This book is designed for students who have mastered some of the basics of English in the skill areas of listening, speaking, reading, and writing but who still need to become more fully functional in everyday activities. Specifically, the contents presuppose student knowledge of the following basic English structures: simple present tense; present continuous; *going to* + verb for the future; imperatives; *can, want* and *need* + *to* + verb. These structures are reviewed in Unit One.

The book is divided into eight units. Each unit contains a general consumer-education theme. The language material in each unit is covered against the background of the unit's consumer theme. Therefore, as students are being introduced to English-language material, they are also being exposed to consumer information that they need in order to function competently in American society. This dual focus on developing linguistic competence and functional consumer competence is the distinguishing characteristic of this book.

Key features of the units include the following:

Learner objectives, which specify the target consumer and language competencies of each unit as well as the vocabulary items.

Dialogues, which introduce consumer topics and target structures to be covered in the unit.

Comprehension questions on the dialogues reinforcing the consumer theme of the unit and the target structures.

Grammar practice in communicative and functional contexts related to the consumer theme of the unit. Exercises are varied and proceed from controlled types to less controlled types. Simplified grammatical explanations with examples are provided.

Reading exercises focusing on basic consumer information and reinforcing target grammatical material.

Listening comprehension exercises designed to help students develop aural skills necessary for functioning effectively as a consumer.

Problem-solving activities in selected units that require the student to tap language and consumer knowledge simultaneously in order to make prudent consumer decisions.

In an easy-to-use format, *Everyday Consumer English* contains a variety of stimulating communicative activities aimed at improving speaking, reading, writing, and listening skills, all in the context of general consumer themes.

Unit One

$ Budgets

Learner Objectives

Consumer Competencies

Learning what a budget is
Learning how to plan a family or individual
    budget
Learning how to use a budget

Grammatical Structures

Review of the following structures: simple
    present tense; present continuous;
    going to + verb for the future;
    imperatives
Being able to understand and use the
    following structures: *can, want,* and
    need + to + verb

Vocabulary Items

Being able to understand and use the following words in context:

Nouns		*Verbs*
accident	Laundromat	average
ad	laundry	budget
advertisement	lease	complain
amount	loan	confuse
appliance	payment	decrease
architect	repair	include
average	steak	register
bank account	take-home pay	rent
bill	tax	save
budget	washing machine	spend
consumer		
dryer	*Adjectives*	
emergency	angry	
expense	medical	
insurance		

Reading

Michael's in the public library. He's putting up an advertisement about a class in consumer education. He's going to teach the Consumer Education class. Michael's going to put up the ad in many places—in supermarkets, shopping centers, Laundromats, and at the university. Tomorrow the ad is going to be in the newspaper.

Here's the ad:

Do you spend a lot of money every month?

Do you get angry about the high cost of living?

Do you know how to open a bank account, rent an apartment, buy furniture?

Do advertisements and leases confuse you?

Come to the
Consumer Education class
You can learn to:

- Budget your money.
- Spend less and save more.
- Save money at the supermarket.
- Rent an apartment.
- Buy furniture and appliances.
- Understand advertisements and leases.

You can learn to be
a good consumer!

TIME: 8–10 p.m., Tuesdays and Thursdays

PLACE: Continental Community College

Call Continental Community College to register.

PHONE: 654-7900

Comprehension Questions

1. What's a consumer? Who's a consumer?

2. Where's Michael?

3. What's he doing?

4. Who's going to teach the Consumer Education class?

5. Where's Michael going to put up the ad?

6. What can you learn in the Consumer Education class?

7. When and where's the Consumer Education class?

8. How can you register for the Consumer Education class?

Grammar Practice

Tense Review: Present; Present Continuous; *Going to* + Verb for the Future; Imperatives

A. Read about Cindy.

Cindy's at home. She's watching TV. Her father is reading the newspaper. He sees the ad for the Consumer Education class.

Cindy's father:
Cindy, here's a class for you and Ron. It's a good class to take before you get married.

Cindy: *(reading the ad)*
"Learn to budget your money; learn to spend less and save more." Ron and I need this class! I'm going to call him right away. He always complains because he can't save money. Everything is so expensive!

Ask your classmates about their activities. Follow the example. Answer with a short answer.

Example: Cindy's watching TV.
                  Are you watching TV?

                  No, I'm not.

1. Cindy's father is reading the newspaper.
    Are you reading the newspaper?

    Yes I am.

2. Cindy wants to learn to budget her money.
    Do you want to learn to budget your money?

    Yes I do.

3. Ron always complains because he can't save money.
    Do you always complain because you can't save money?

    Yes I do.

B. Read about Ken and Lisa.

Ken and Lisa are shopping at the supermarket. Lisa sees the ad for the Consumer Education class.

Lisa:
Ken, here's the perfect class for us! "Learn to save money at the supermarket."

Ken:
"Learn to budget your money." You're right, Lisa. We need to budget our money. We need to save money for the baby.

Lisa:
Let's register right away.

Ask your classmates about their activities. Follow the examples. Form questions. Answer them with a short answer.

Example: Ken and Lisa are shopping at the supermarket.

                  Are you shopping at the supermarket?

                  No, I'm not.

1. Lisa wants to learn to save money at the supermarket.

   _____?

   _____.

2. Ken wants to learn to budget their money.

   _____?

   _____.

3. Ken and Lisa need to save money for their baby.

   _____?

   _____.

4. Ken and Lisa are going to register for the Consumer Education class.

   _____?

   _____.

C. Read about Barbara.

Barbara's going to paint the kitchen in her apartment. She's putting newspaper on the floor. She sees the ad for the Consumer Education class.

Barbara: *(thinking)*
Hmmm. This class looks interesting. "Learn to rent an apartment. Learn to understand advertisements and leases." I need a new apartment. I'm tired of this one. I always need to paint or fix it. I'm going to register for this class.

Ask your classmates about their activities. Follow the example. Form questions. Answer them with a short answer.

Example: Barbara's going to paint her kitchen.

   Are you going to paint your kitchen?

   Yes, I am.

1. Barbara needs a new apartment.

   _____?

   _____.

2. Barbara's tired of her apartment.

_____?

_____.

3. Barbara always needs to paint or fix her apartment.

_____?

_____.

4. Barbara wants to register for the Consumer Education class.

_____?

_____.

D. Read about budgets.

The Consumer Education class is learning about budgets. A budget is a plan for the use of your money. It can help you spend your money. It can also help you save money.

Barbara's making a budget. How much does she spend a month? Ask questions to find out. Follow the examples.

Example: rent

How much does Barbara spend a month on rent?

$304/month

She spends $304 a month on rent.

1. food

_____?

$80/month

_____.

2. rental insurance

_____?

$60/year $60 ÷ 12 = $____/month

_____.

3. gas for her car

_____?

$15/week $15 × 4 = $____/month

_____.

4. car insurance

_____?

$264/year $264 ÷ 12 = $____/month

_____.

Example: electric bill

_How much is Barbara's electric bill a month?_____

$15.36/month

_Her electric bill is $15.36 a month._____

1. gas bill

_____?

$13.21/month

_____.

2. water bill

_____?

$9.45/two months $9.45 ÷ 2 = $____/month

_____.

3. telephone bill

_____?

$19.64/month

_____.

4. car loan payment

_____?

$130/month

_____.

5. college loan payment

_____?

$30/month

_____.

E. Answer these questions.

1. What bills do you pay every month?

2. What bills are the same every month?

3. What bills change every month?

4. How can you save money?

5. Are you saving money now?

F. Read about Barbara's additional expenses.

Barbara pays some bills once a month, for example, her rent, electric, gas, and water bills. She pays some bills once every two months, for example, her water bill. Barbara pays her car insurance twice a year. In March she pays $132. From April to September she saves $22 a month. So in September, she has $132 to pay her car insurance bill. Barbara pays her rental insurance once a year in April. Every month she saves $5. So in April, she has $60 to pay her rental insurance.

What expenses does Barbara have once a month? Once every two months? Once a year? Twice a year?

Problem Solving

Making a Budget

Make a budget for Barbara. Write down her expenses.

EXPENSES	AMOUNT PER MONTH
rent	$304
food	80
rental insurance	
gas for her car	
car insurance	
electricity	
gas	
water	
telephone	
car loan payment	
college loan payment	
OTHER EXPENSES:	
TOTAL	
Barbara's take-home pay: $382.96/two weeks × 2 =	

Now make a budget for yourself. Write down your expenses. How much do you spend a month for rent, food, electricity, and other necessities?

Grammar Practice

Can, Want, and *Need* + *to* + Verb

A. Read some more about Barbara.

Barbara needs to save money. She needs four new tires for her car. They cost about $120. She needs to buy them within three months. She's saving money for them.

Barbara wants to save money. She wants to buy a new TV. She wants a color TV, but color TV's are very expensive. She's going to save her money for a long time. She's going to save money for a color TV.

How can Barbara save money? Give her suggestions. Use *can.* Follow the example.

Example: Barbara eats lunch at a restaurant at least twice a week.

She can take her lunch.

She can eat at a restaurant only once a week.

1. Barbara goes to the movies twice a month.

    _____ go only once a month.

    _____ go in the afternoon. It's cheaper then.

2. Barbara drives to work every day. It costs her $15 a week for gas and $7.50 a week for parking.

    She can_____.

    She can_____.

3. Barbara goes hiking in the country twice a month. She drives about 200 miles each time.

    She can_____.

    She can_____.

4. Barbara makes long-distance calls to her parents and friends every week.

    She can_____.

    She can_____.

5. Barbara likes to buy books. She buys a new book every week.

    She can_____.

    She can_____.

6. Barbara has her own apartment. The rent is $304 a month.

She can_____.

She can_____.

B. Ken and Lisa want to have a baby. They're saving for the baby. They need to buy a washing machine and a dryer. Answer the questions about Ken and Lisa. Follow the example.

Example: Ken and Lisa usually go to the movies every Saturday night. But they want to save money. It's Saturday night. What are they doing?

*They're watching TV.*_____

1. Ken and Lisa usually eat at a restaurant every Friday night. But they want to save money. It's Friday night. What are they doing?

_____.

2. Ken likes to have steak once a week for dinner. But steak is expensive, and Ken and Lisa want to save money. What are they eating for dinner tonight?

_____.

3. Ken and Lisa like to go to a baseball game about two or three times a month during the summer. But the tickets are expensive, and Ken and Lisa want to save money. Tonight there's a baseball game. What are Ken and Lisa doing?

_____.

C. Form questions with the following phrases. Answer them. Use the present tense. Follow the example.

Example: pay your rent   (when)

*When do you pay your rent?*_____

*I pay my rent on the first day of every month.*_____

1. pay your telephone bill   (when)

_____?

_____.

2. spend a week on food   (how much)

_____?

_____.

3. need to buy this year   (what)

_____?

_____.

4. want to buy this year   (what)

_____?

_____.

5. save a month   (how much)

_____?

_____.

D. Complete these conversations. Follow the example.

Example: Ron: I can't save money.

Cindy: You need to _make a budget._ _____

1. Lisa: We need to save money for the baby.

Ken: We can_____.

2. Jane: Let's go out to lunch today.

Barbara: No,_____.

3. Barbara: I always need to paint or fix my apartment.

Jane:_____.

4. Barbara:_____.

Jane: You need to save money for a long time.

5. Lisa: Let's go to the movies tonight.

Ken: No,_____.

Reading

Do you want to save money? You can make a budget and save money. It's important to know how much money you spend a month. Some expenses are the same every month, for example, rent, car loan payments, and car insurance. But some expenses change every month. For example, let's say during the winter you use a lot of gas to heat your home. Then your gas bill is very high. In the summer you don't heat your home. Then your gas bill is low. You spend a different amount each month on gas for your home.

You can average your expenses. For example, let's say in June you spend $60 for gas for your car. In July you spend $55. In August you take a trip during the weekend. You spend $100 for gas for your car in August.

June	$ 60	
July	55	
August	100	$215 ÷ 3 = $71.67
	$215	

You spend an average of $71.67 a month for gas for your car for these three months.

It's important to save money for emergencies. Let's say you and your husband or wife work. Your husband or wife has an accident and can't work for two months. What can you do? How can you pay your bills? You can save money every month for emergencies. It's important to include money for emergencies in your budget.

Comprehension Questions

Write the answers to the following questions.

1. How can you save money?

2. Which expenses are the same every month?

3. Which expenses change every month?

4. Why is it important to average your expenses?

5. What are some possible emergencies?

6. Do you have money for emergencies?

Listening Comprehension

A. Fill in the blanks with the amounts that your teacher says. Remember to use the dollar sign.

Ken and Lisa want to make a budget. Ken's an architect. His take-home pay is _____ a month. Lisa works at a university. Her take-home pay is _____ a month. Their house payment is _____ a month. They have home insurance. It costs _____ a year. Taxes on their house cost _____ a year. Their gas, electric, and water bills are about _____ a month. The telephone is about _____ a month. Ken drives to work. Gas costs about _____ a week. Parking costs _____ a week. Lisa takes the bus. She spends _____ a week. They have car insurance. It costs _____ a year. Their car loan payment is _____ a month. Repairs on their car cost about _____ a year. Ken and Lisa spend about _____ a week on food. Their medical expenses are about _____ a year.

Ken likes to buy clothes. He spends about _____ a month on clothes. Lisa likes to go to the movies every week. The movies cost _____ a week.

B. Listen to the story above again. Answer these questions.

1. What other expenses do Ken and Lisa have?

2. Ken and Lisa want to have a baby. They want to save money for the baby. How much can they save each week?

Problem Solving

Making a Budget

Make a budget for Ken and Lisa based on the information in the Listening Comprehension exercise. What other expenses do Ken and Lisa have? How much can they save each month?

EXPENSES	AMOUNT PER MONTH
House payment	
Home insurance	
House taxes	
Gas, electricity, water	
Telephone	
Gas for their car	
Parking	
Bus	
Car insurance	
Car loan payment	
Car repairs	
Food	
Medical expenses	
Clothes	
Movies	
OTHER EXPENSES:	
TOTAL EXPENSES	
Ken's take-home pay	
Lisa's take-home pay	
TOTAL TAKE-HOME PAY	

Meeting Expenses

Work in groups to solve these problems. Write down your answers. Discuss your answers with the rest of the class.

1. Ken and Lisa want to have a baby. They want to buy a washing machine and dryer soon. How can they save money? How can they decrease their expenses?

2. Let's say Ken and Lisa's refrigerator stops working. It costs $150 to repair it or $500 to buy a new one. How can they save money? How can they decrease their expenses?

3. Let's say after Ken and Lisa have their baby, Lisa doesn't want to work. She wants to stay home with the baby for a year. Can they pay their bills?

4. Ken and Lisa want to save money for their child's education. How much can they save a month?

Unit Two

 # Banking— Savings Accounts

Learner Objectives

Consumer Competencies

Becoming familiar with and being able to use banking services such as savings accounts

Grammatical Structures

Being able to understand and use the following structures: the past tense and *should*

Vocabulary Items

Being able to understand and use the following words in context:

Nouns
account
bank manager
bill
car mechanic
change
checking account
clerk
credit card
coin
department store
deposit
deposit slip

interest
interest rate
loan
passbook
paycheck
robber
savings account
savings and loan
   association
signature card
social security
   number
withdrawal slip

Verbs
check
deposit
earn
fix
insure
lose
print
repair
rob
save
sign
withdraw

Adjectives
convenient
minimum

Dialogue

Ron and Cindy are going to get married soon. They're reading the Sunday newspaper. Cindy's looking at the department store ads.

Cindy:
Ron, look at these towels. Aren't they beautiful!

Ron:
Yes, they're nice, but expensive.

Cindy:
I want to buy so many things for our apartment—sheets, towels, furniture, dishes.

Ron:
We need a lot of things. We should start saving money.

Cindy:
Maybe we should open a savings account together. Look, Ron, here's an ad for a bank. You open a savings account, and they give you a free gift.

Ron:
Let's see. But Cindy, the minimum deposit is $1,000. And besides, this bank is on the other side of town. We should open an account at a bank nearby. We can call a few banks tomorrow and ask about savings accounts.

Comprehension Questions

1. What are Ron and Cindy doing?

2. What's Cindy looking at?

3. What does Cindy want to buy?

4. What should Ron and Cindy do to save money?

5. How can you get a free gift?

6. Where's the bank?

7. Where should they open an account?

8. What are Ron and Cindy going to do?

Reading

Ron and Cindy decided to open a savings account at Fidelity Bank. Fidelity Bank is convenient for them because it's near Ron's apartment. It's open late on Fridays, so they can go there after work.

Yesterday they went to the bank. They asked the bank manager about savings accounts. They decided to open a regular passbook savings account. That means they can deposit (put in) or withdraw (take out) their money any time. First they signed a signature card. The signature card shows the bank how they sign their names. On the signature card they printed their name, address, social security number, occupation, and their employer's address. Ron and Cindy deposited $200 in their account. The bank manager typed the amount "$200" in a passbook. He also typed Cindy's name and Ron's name and their new account number. He gave them the passbook.

Fidelity Bank pays 5¼% interest on regular passbook savings accounts. It pays interest every day. That means that Cindy and Ron can deposit or withdraw money any time, and they don't lose interest. Every time Cindy and Ron deposit money in their savings account or withdraw money from their savings account, they need their passbook.

Comprehension Questions

Write the answers to the following questions.

1. Where did Ron and Cindy decide to open a savings account? Why?

2. What kind of account did they open? Why?

3. What did they do first?

4. What's a signature card?

5. What did they write on the signature card?

6. How much did they deposit?

7. What did the bank manager type in the passbook?

8. How much interest does Fidelity Bank pay on regular passbook savings accounts?

9. How often do they pay interest?

10. What do Cindy and Ron need when they deposit or withdraw money?

Problem Solving

Signature Cards

This is the signature card that Ron and Cindy filled out to open their savings account.

Joint Tenancy	ACCOUNT NO. 939-5257910

Ronald Evans
SIGNATURE

SOCIAL SECURITY NUMBER
6 5 4 | 1 2 | 3 4 5 0

Cynthia S Hudson
SIGNATURE

SOCIAL SECURITY NUMBER
9 8 7 | 4 5 | 6 3 2 7

We, whose signatures appear above, hereby jointly and severally agree and declare that we are joint owners in joint tenancy of all the money that is now or may hereafter be deposited in The Fidelity Bank of Pittsburgh in our names, and of any interest that may accrue thereon or be credited thereto, and that either of us may withdraw by check or other order of withdrawal the whole or any part thereof, and that upon the death of either of us the balance in said account shall belong absolutely to the survivor who shall be sole owner thereof, as surviving joint tenant, such survivor being hereby authorized to receive the same from said Bank on his or her individual check or other order of withdrawal therefor.

Each of us hereby grants to the other full power and authority to endorse, by written signature or otherwise, all checks, drafts and other instruments drawn or payable to the order of either of us, or to our joint order, for deposit in this account.

In the case of overdraft by either of us or overpayment to either, whether by error, mistake, inadvertance or otherwise, we are jointly and severally liable to the bank for said overdraft or overpayment.

This agreement is not revocable except by notice in writing by both parties hereto.

FIDELITY BANK
Pittsburgh, PA

_3-6-91_
DATE

1104-D REV. 76

NAME _Ronald Evans_ (412) 655-4526 PHONE

RESIDENCE _412 40th St. Pittsburgh, PA 15222_

OCCUPATION _car mechanic_ (412) 552-0205 PHONE

BUSINESS ADDRESS _102 Center St._

NAME _Cynthia S. Hudson_ _friend_ RELATIONSHIP

RESIDENCE _5822 College Ave. Pittsburgh, PA 15223_

OCCUPATION _bookkeeper_ (412) 532-5300 PHONE

BUSINESS ADDRESS _711 5th St._

IDENTIFICATION REMARKS

OVER

Now fill out a signature card to open an individual savings account.

INDIVIDUAL	ACCOUNT No.

SIGNATURE

SOCIAL SECURITY NUMBER

PHONE NUMBER

RESIDENCE

OCCUPATION

BUSINESS
ADDRESS

INTRODUCED BY

DATE

FIDELITY BANK

1104-A

Deposit Slips

Ron and Cindy deposited a $25 check and $10 cash in their savings account. Fill out the deposit slip for them.

DEPOSITED WITH
FIDELITY BANK
FOR CREDIT TO THE REGULAR SAVINGS
ACCOUNT NAMED HEREON

DATE _____ 19 ____

NAME _____
WRITE ACCOUNT NAME ABOVE

C. C. 3—5
OFFICE #

C. C. 6—12
ACCOUNT NO.

RB — 504 REV. (8-76)

	DOLLARS	CENTS
CASH		
CHECKS, PLEASE LIST SEPARATELY SHOWING THE BANK'S TRANSIT NUMBER		
TOTAL		

REGULAR SAVINGS DEPOSIT

FIDELITY BANK

This is their passbook after they made the deposit.

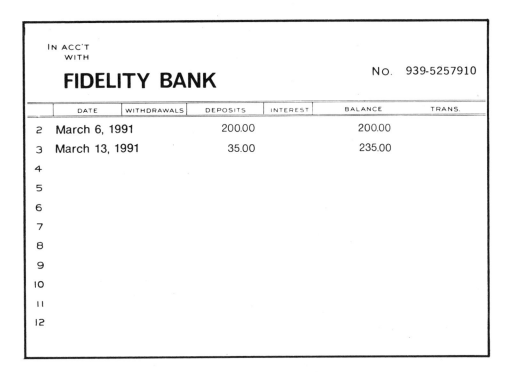

	DATE	WITHDRAWALS	DEPOSITS	INTEREST	BALANCE	TRANS.
	IN ACC'T WITH					
	FIDELITY BANK			No. 939-5257910		
2	March 6, 1991		200.00		200.00	
3	March 13, 1991		35.00		235.00	
4						
5						
6						
7						
8						
9						
10						
11						
12						

Withdrawal Slips

Lisa withdrew $13.50 cash from her savings account. Fill out the withdrawal slip for her.

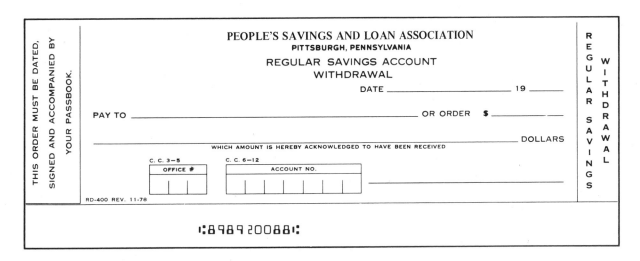

THIS ORDER MUST BE DATED, SIGNED AND ACCOMPANIED BY YOUR PASSBOOK.

PEOPLE'S SAVINGS AND LOAN ASSOCIATION
PITTSBURGH, PENNSYLVANIA
REGULAR SAVINGS ACCOUNT
WITHDRAWAL

DATE _____ 19 _____

PAY TO _____ OR ORDER $ _____

_____ DOLLARS
WHICH AMOUNT IS HEREBY ACKNOWLEDGED TO HAVE BEEN RECEIVED

C. C. 3—5   C. C. 6—12
OFFICE #   ACCOUNT NO.

RD-400 REV. 11-78

REGULAR SAVINGS WITHDRAWAL

⑆898920088⑆

Grammar Practice

Past Tense

One way to form the past tense is to add *ed* to the simple form of regular verbs. If the simple form ends in *e,* we add only *d* (smoke → smoked).

I work*ed* yesterday	We work*ed* yesterday.
You work*ed* yesterday.	You work*ed* yesterday.
He, she, it, work*ed* yesterday.	They work*ed* yesterday.

We use *did* in affirmative questions and affirmative short answers to show past time. We use the simple form of the verb after *did* in affirmative questions.

Question Form

Did	Subject	Verb (simple form)	Complement
Did	Ron	work	yesterday?
Where did	Ron	go	yesterday?

Short Answer

Yes, he did.

In negative questions, negative statements, and negative short answers we use *didn't (did + not).* We use the simple form of the verb after *didn't,* except in short answers.

Question Form

Didn't Did + Not	Subject	Verb (simple form)	Complement
Didn't	Ron	work	yesterday?

Statement form

Subject	Didn't Did + Not	Verb (simple form)	Complement
Ron	didn't	work	yesterday.

Short Answer

No, he didn't.

We use these expressions to show past time:

last night, last week, last month, last year, last Sunday;

three days ago, two years ago, a week ago;

yesterday, yesterday morning, yesterday afternoon, yesterday evening.

Irregular Verbs

Many common verbs are irregular in the past tense. These are used in this unit:

Simple present tense	Past tense	Simple present tense	Past tense
be	was, were	make	made
buy	bought	pay	paid
catch	caught	read	read
get	got	spend	spent
give	gave	withdraw	withdrew
go	went	write	wrote
have	had		

Note the past tense of the verb *be:*

I was	we were
you were	you were
he, she, it was	they were

Question Form

Were you at the game yesterday?

Wasn't he sick yesterday?

Short Answer

Yes, I was.

No, he wasn't.

Past Tense: Exercises

A. Fill in the blanks with the past tense form of the verb. Follow the example.

Example: The Consumer Education class _discussed_ (discuss) banking.

1. We _____ (open) a savings account two months ago.

2. Lisa and Ken _____ (save) $50 last month.

3. You _____ (wash) the dishes after dinner last night.

4. The Consumer Education class _____ (talk) about budgets last week.

5. I _____ (ask) the bank manager about savings accounts.

B. Fill in the blanks with the past tense form of the verb. These verbs are irregular. Follow the example.

Example: I *withdrew* (withdraw) $50 from my savings account two days ago.

1. Lisa and Ken _____ (make) a budget last week.

2. They _____ (write) down their expenses yesterday morning.

3. Ken and Lisa _____ (spend) $7 a week last year for the movies.

4. The bank _____ (pay) 5% interest last year on savings accounts.

5. You _____ (get) a package in the mail yesterday.

C. Form *yes/no* questions in the past tense. Answer them with a short answer. Follow the example.

Example: *Did the students talk* (the students/talk) about banking last week?

      Yes, they did.

1. _____ (you/go) shopping this morning?

   _____.

2. _____ (Ken and Lisa/need) to save money last year?

   _____.

3. _____ (we/receive) any mail yesterday?

   _____.

4. _____ (you/fill) out a signature card to open a savings account?

   _____.

5. _____ (Cindy and Ron/deposit) $200 in their savings account last week?

   _____.

D. Form questions in the past tense. Answer them. Follow the example.

Example: Where _did Cindy and Ron go_ (Cindy and Ron/go) Friday after work?

They went to the bank.

1. Why _____ (you/need) to save money last year?

   _____.

2. Why _____ (you/decide) to open a savings account?

   _____.

3. Where _____ (you/open) a bank account?

   _____.

4. How much interest _____ (your bank/pay) on savings accounts last year?

   _____.

5. When _____ (you/deposit) your paycheck in your bank account?

   _____.

E. This is what Michael did in the evenings last week. Answer the questions according to the example.

Sunday	Monday	Tuesday	Wednesday
stay home	play tennis	go to class	watch TV

Thursday	Friday	Saturday
go to class	go to a baseball game	go to the movies

Example: Did Michael eat dinner at a restaurant Sunday evening?

No, he didn't. He stayed home.

1. Did Michael read a book Monday evening?

2. Did Michael go to the movies Tuesday evening?

3. Did Michael go to class Wednesday evening?

4. Did Michael wash his car Thursday evening?

5. Did Michael go to a party Friday evening?

6. Did Michael go bowling Saturday evening?

F. Form *yes/no* questions in the past tense with the following phrases. Answer them. Follow the example.

Example: pay the telephone bill

Did you pay the telephone bill last month?
No, I didn't.

1. open a savings account

2. make a budget

3. save money for emergencies

4. go to class

5. deposit money in your savings account

G. Form questions in the past tense with the following phrases. Answer them. Follow the example.

Example: pay the telephone bill (when)

When did you pay the telephone bill?
I paid it yesterday.

1. withdraw $75 (why)

2. go shopping (when)

3. go last night (where)

4. make a budget (why)

5. buy a new shirt (when)

H. Rewrite this story in the past tense. Change *tonight* and *at night* to *that night*.

It's morning. Fred, a bank robber, plans to rob the Second National Bank tonight. First, he makes a budget. He wants to know how much money he needs to rob. He writes down his expenses. Every time he robs a bank, he needs to get a gun, tools, a mask, a get-away car, and gas. He also needs money to go to the annual Bank Robbers Convention in Chicago. Next, he writes down his emergency expenses. For example, he needs money to hire a lawyer if the police catch him.

Then he goes shopping to buy supplies for the bank robbery. He buys a gun, tools, a bag for the money, and a mask. He also buys a used car. He pays for everything with his credit card. He makes a map of the streets around the bank and another map of the inside of the bank.

At night he robs the bank. The next day he goes to the First National Bank. He deposits his money in a savings account. He wants to earn interest. He doesn't worry about bank robbers. The First National Bank insures savings accounts!

I.   This is a typical day for Lisa and Ron.

Lisa's a university professor. She works five days a week. Sometimes she works on the weekends. At 10:00 a.m. she has a class. At 12:30 she goes to lunch. Sometimes she goes to a restaurant with other professors or students. She buys a sandwich. In the afternoon she prepares for her classes. She usually goes home about 4:30 p.m.

Ron's a car mechanic. He works five days a week. He goes to work at 7:30 a.m. He starts work at 8:00. He repairs cars all day. He fixes motors. He changes tires. At 10:30 he gets a coffee break. At noon he has lunch. He goes home at 5:00 p.m. He always buys an evening paper on the way home. When he gets home, he washes his face and hands and then has dinner. In the evening he watches TV or goes out with Cindy.

Yesterday was a typical day for Lisa and Ron. Tell the class what they did.

Now tell the class what you do on a typical day. Tell the class what you did yesterday.

J.   Here is some information about Barbara. Talk about Barbara. Talk about her education and experience.

Barbara

Education

Central High School	1971-1974
University of Pittsburgh	
B.A., Spanish	1974-1978

Travel

Mexico	6 months, 1977

Employment

waitress	summers, 1973, 1974
recreation counselor city park program	summers, 1975, 1976
office worker	part-time, 1977-1978
travel agent	1978-present

Now make a chart about yourself and the other students in the class. Talk about your education and experience.

K. Complete these conversations in the past tense.

1. Did you open_____
at People's Savings and Loan Association?

No,_____.

2. What time_____yesterday?

8:00.

3. How much_____?

$35.

4. _____?

We had hamburgers, potato chips, and soft drinks.

5. Did you go to class last night?

No,_____.

Should

Should usually refers to the present or future. It is followed by the simple form of the verb.

Should expresses a suggestion. In the affirmative it means that it is advisable to do something, for example, *The students should do their homework.*
    Shouldn't means that it is advisable *not* to do something, for example, *You shouldn't smoke so much.*
    Questions with *should* are used to ask for advice or suggestions, for example, *Should I open an account at First National Bank or at Fidelity Bank?*

	Subject	Should	Verb (simple form)	Complement
Affirmative	Ron	should	open	a savings account.
Negative	Ron	should not shouldn't	keep	his money at home.

	Should	Subject	Verb (simple form)	Complement
Question Form	Should	Cindy	open	a savings account?
Short Answer	Yes, she should. No, she shouldn't.			

Should: **Exercises**

A. Read the following dialogue. Barbara is talking to her friend José from Ecuador.

Barbara:
Hi, José. How are you?

José:
Terrible.

Barbara:
What's wrong?

José:
Someone robbed my apartment last week. The robber took $350.

Barbara:
Oh, no! Did you call the police?

José:
No.

Barbara:
Why not?

José:
My English isn't very good. I didn't know what to say to them.

Barbara:
I'm going to give you some advice, José. If this happens again, you should call the police immediately. You should try to remember everything. You should explain everything to the police.

José:
That's difficult for a foreigner.

Barbara:
Then you should ask me to help you. Do you always keep your money at home?

José:
Yes, I keep it in a box in my bedroom.

Barbara:
Oh, no! José, you should open a savings account. You shouldn't keep your money at home. Let's go to the bank right now.

B. Answer these questions based on the dialogue.

  1. What happened to José last week?

  2. How much did the robber take?

  3. Did José call the police? Why not?

C. Answer these questions with short answers. Refer to the dialogue.

  1. Should José call the police?

  2. Should he explain everything to the police?

  3. Should he ask Barbara to help him?

  4. Should he keep his money at home?

  5. Should he go to the bank to find out about savings accounts?

  6. Should he open a savings account?

D. Fill in the blanks with *should* and the verb. Follow the example.

Example: José *should open* (open) a savings account.

1. Before you open a savings account, you _____ (call) several banks and savings and loan associations.

2. You _____ (ask) for information about savings accounts because there are many different plans for saving.

3. You _____ (find) out the interest rates.

4. You _____ (save) money for emergencies.

5. You _____ (make) a budget.

E. Fill in the blanks with *shouldn't* and the verb.

Example: José *shouldn't keep* (keep) a lot of money at home.

1. You _____ (be) late for work.

2. Cindy _____ (spend) all her money.

3. Barbara _____ (pay) her bills late.

4. José _____ (carry) a lot of cash in his pocket.

5. You _____ (forget) your passbook when you go to the bank.

F. Form *yes/no* questions with *should* and the following phrases. Write a short answer. Follow the example.

Example: open a savings account

　　　　　　　　Should Ron and Cindy open a savings account?

　　　　　　　　Yes, they should.

1. save money

2. buy a new car

3. take an umbrella

4. go to the doctor

5. come to class on time

G. Complete these conversations. Use *should,* if possible.

Example: *Should we open an account* at First National Bank or Fidelity Bank?

Fidelity Bank. It's close to our house.

1. How much_____in our savings account?

_____.

2. I have a terrible headache!

You should_____.

3. What time_____?

Come at 2:00.

4. Oh, no! I gained two pounds!

_____.

5. _____?

I should do it, but I don't want to.

H. Give advice about the following situations. Use *should* or *shouldn't.*

Example: José keeps his money under the bed.

He should open a bank account.
He shouldn't keep his money at home.

1. Someone robbed José's apartment.

2. Cindy and Ron want to save money.

3. It's cold outside.

4. The phone is ringing.

5. My clothes are dirty.

Listening Comprehension

A. Listen to your teacher. Write the numbers that you hear.

1. _____ _____ _____ _____ _____ _____ _____ _____

   How much did Barbara withdraw? _____

2. _____ _____ _____ _____ _____ _____ _____ _____

   How much did Barbara withdraw? _____

3. _____ _____ _____ _____ _____ _____ _____ _____

   How much did Barbara withdraw? _____

4. _____ _____ _____ _____ _____ _____ _____ _____

   How much did Barbara withdraw? _____

5. _____ _____ _____ _____ _____ _____ _____ _____

   How much did Barbara withdraw? _____

B. Listen to your teacher. Write the numbers that you hear.

1. Michael's at a department store. He's buying a pair of blue jeans. They cost _____. He gives the clerk _____. The clerk is counting out his change. Write the numbers that you hear.

   _____ _____ _____ _____

How much change did the clerk give Michael?_____

What coins and bills did the clerk give Michael?_____

_____

2. Ken's at a fast-food restaurant. He gets a hamburger, French fries, and a chocolate

   milkshake. They cost _____. He gives the clerk _____. The clerk is counting out

   his change. Write the numbers that you hear.

   _____ _____ _____ _____

   How much change did the clerk give Ken?_____

   What coins did the clerk give Ken?_____

   _____

3. Lisa's at the supermarket. Her food costs _____. Lisa gives the clerk _____. The

   clerk is counting out her change. Write the numbers that you hear.

   _____ _____ _____ _____ _____ _____ _____

   How much change did the clerk give Lisa?_____

   What coins and bills did the clerk give Lisa?_____

   _____

Reading

Choosing a Bank or Savings and Loan Association

In the Consumer Education class the students read the following information about choosing a bank or savings and loan association.

You should choose a bank or savings and loan association very carefully. You should check many things before you open a bank account. Here are some things you should look for:

Location You should be sure the bank or savings and loan association is convenient. It should be near your house or your job.

Hours You should be sure the bank or savings and loan association is open when you can go there. For example, let's say you work from 8 a.m. to 5 p.m. You should find a bank or savings and loan association near your home that's open on Saturdays or after 5 p.m. during the week. Or you should find a bank or savings and loan association near your job. Then you can go during your lunch hour.

Services
Savings Accounts

Banks and savings and loan associations have different types of savings plans and pay interest in different ways. Savings and loan associations usually pay more interest than banks. You should check the interest rate on the different savings plans. Compare these two plans:

The interest rate for regular passbook savings accounts at First National Bank is 5¼%. First National Bank pays interest every six months. Let's say you open a savings account on January 2 and deposit $500. On March 30, you withdraw $200. On June 30 the First National Bank pays you interest on $300. It doesn't pay you interest on the $200 because you withdrew it before June 30. On June 30 you have $300 and $7.88 interest.

The interest rate for regular passbook savings accounts at People's Savings and Loan Association is 5½%. People's Savings and Loan Association pays interest every day. Let's say you open a savings account on January 2 and deposit $500. On March 30 you withdraw $200. People's Savings and Loan pays you interest every day on the $500 until March 30. After March 30 it pays you interest on $300. So, on June 30 you have $300 and $11.17 interest.

Checking Accounts

Banks offer checking accounts; savings and loan associations usually do not. A checking account is a safe way to pay your bills, rent, etc. You put money in your account. You write checks to a person or place to spend the money in your checking account. The check tells the bank to pay a specific amount of money from your account to the person or place.

Loans

Both banks and savings and loan associations offer loans.

Credit Cards

Banks offer credit cards; savings and loan associations usually do not.

You should be sure the bank is a member of the Federal Deposit Insurance Corporation (F.D.I.C.) and the savings and loan association a member of the Federal Savings and Loan Insurance Corporation (F.S.L.I.C.). The F.D.I.C. and the F.S.L.I.C. insure your money. This means if there's a fire or if someone robs the bank, you do not lose your money.

Comprehension Questions

Write the answers to the following questions.

1. Why should the bank or savings and loan association be near your job or house?

2. Does a bank or a savings and loan association usually pay more interest on regular passbook savings accounts?

3. How often does First National Bank pay interest? How often does People's Savings and Loan Association pay interest? Do you prefer First National Bank's plan for savings accounts or People's Savings and Loan Association's plan for savings accounts? Why?

4. What is a checking account?

5. What services do banks offer? What services do savings and loan associations offer?

6. Why should a bank be a member of the F.D.I.C. and a savings and loan association a member of the F.S.L.I.C.?

Problem Solving

Compare First National Bank and People's Savings and Loan Association. Where should you open a savings account? Which place is better for you? Why?

	First National Bank	People's Savings and Loan Association
Location	near your home	near your job
Hours	9 a.m. – 4 p.m. Monday – Wednesday, Friday 9 a.m. – 8 p.m. Thursday	9 a.m. – 4 p.m. Monday – Thursday 9 a.m. – 6 p.m. Friday
Interest rates (on regular passbook savings accounts)	5¼% paid every 6 months	5½% paid everyday
Other Services	checking accounts, loans, credit cards	loans
	member F.D.I.C.	member F.S.L.I.C.

Unit Three

Banking—Checking Accounts

Learner Objectives

Consumer Competencies

Becoming familiar with and being able to use banking services, for example, checking accounts and credit cards
Beginning to develop an understanding of the basic principles of credit systems

Grammatical Structures

Being able to understand and use the following structures: the past continuous tense and *must* and *have to.*

Vocabulary Items

Being able to understand and use the following words in context:

Nouns	teller	*Adjective*
balance	vending machine	canceled
bank statement		
billing date	*Verbs*	
cash	afford	
charge form	apply	
check	bounce	
checkbook	cash	
customer	charge	
identification	deduct	
purchase	disappear	
receipt	endorse	
record	fill out	
service charge	run into	

Dialogue

Yesterday Cindy and Ron were walking in the park when suddenly. . .

Cindy:
Oh, no! Ron, where's my purse?

Ron:
Don't you have it?

Cindy:
I did, but it disappeared!

Ron:
Cindy, purses don't just disappear. Think carefully. When did you have it last?

Cindy:
I had it when I left the house . . . I had it when we stopped to get a hot dog.

Ron:
OK. Let's go back to the hot dog stand.

(They find the purse at the hot dog stand.)

Cindy: *(looking in her wallet)*
Thank goodness. It's still here. I was really worried.

Ron:
Cindy, why are you carrying so much money?

Cindy:
It's from my paycheck. I cashed it today.

Ron:
You're carrying your whole paycheck in your purse? Why didn't you deposit it in your checking account?

Cindy:
I don't have a checking account. I don't know anything about checking accounts.

Ron:
Cindy, you have to open an account. It's not safe to carry all that cash. Do it tomorrow.

Comprehension Questions

1. What happened when Cindy and Ron were walking in the park?

2. Where did Cindy leave her purse?

3. Was her money still in her purse?

4. How much money was Cindy carrying in her purse?

5. Why was she carrying so much money?

6. Why didn't Cindy deposit her paycheck in her checking account?

7. What did Ron tell her to do? Why?

Grammar Practice

Past Continuous Tense

We form the past continuous tense with the past tense of the verb *be (was, were)* and the *ing*-form of the verb (*talking, running, sleeping*).

Affirmative

Subject	Be	V+*ing*	Complement
Ron and Cindy	were	walking	in the park yesterday afternoon.

Negative

Ron	wasn't	reading	a book yesterday afternoon.

Question Form

Be	Subject	V+*ing*	Complement
Were	Ron and Cindy	walking	in the park yesterday afternoon?
Where were	Ron and Cindy	walking	yesterday afternoon?

Short Answer

Yes, they were.   No, they weren't.

We use the past continuous tense to describe a continuing action at a specific time in the past:

I was reading a book yesterday afternoon.

We also use the past continuous tense with *when* and the past tense to describe two past actions.

In the following sentences, which action came first?

> Cindy and Ron were walking in the park when it started to rain.
> When it started to rain, Cindy and Ron were walking in the park.

The sudden action "it started to rain" interrupts, or comes after, the continuous action "Cindy and Ron were walking in the park."

Now compare the following sentences:

> What were you doing when the fire began?
> I was sleeping.

> What did you do when the fire began?
> I called the fire department.

In the first pair of sentences, the fire began after the subject began sleeping; in the second pair, first the fire began and then the subject called the fire department.

Past Continuous Tense: Exercises

A. Tell what Ken was doing yesterday. Follow the example.

Example: 7:00 a.m.

sleep

At 7:00 Ken was sleeping.

8:00 a.m.	10:00 a.m.	10:30 a.m.	12:30 p.m.
eat breakfast	cut the grass	talk to his neighbor	eat lunch

2:00 p.m.	6:30 p.m.	8:00 p.m.
swim	take a shower	eat dinner at a restaurant

Now tell what you were doing at these times yesterday.

B. Here's what Michael was doing yesterday at different times in the day. Answer the questions. Follow the example.

8:00 a.m.	10:00 a.m.	noon	4:00 p.m.
sleep	eat breakfast	play tennis	walk in the park

6:00 p.m.	8:30 p.m.
eat dinner	watch TV

Example: Was Michael eating breakfast at 8:00 a.m.?

No, he wasn't. He was sleeping.

1. Was Michael cleaning his apartment at 10:00 a.m.?

2. Was Michael eating lunch at noon?

3. Was Michael taking a shower at 4:00 p.m.?

4. Was Michael shopping at 6:00 p.m.?

5. Was Michael dancing at a party at 8:30 p.m.?

C. Cindy went to the bank a few days ago. Tell what was happening when she entered the bank. Follow the example.

Example: woman/deposit money

When Cindy entered the bank, a woman was depositing money.

1. man/cash a check

2. customers/wait in line

3. man and woman/apply for a loan

4. children/wait for their mother

5. teller/talk to a customer

6. woman/fill out a deposit slip

7. guard/look out the window

8. bank manager/talk on the phone

D. Fill in the blank with the correct form of the verb.

Example: The children *were walking* (walk) to school yesterday when it *began* (begin) to rain.

1. The Consumer Education class _____ (discuss) bank accounts when

Barbara _____ (enter) the room.

2. When Ron _____ (call), Cindy _____ (wash) her hair.

3. Barbara _____ (shop) in the supermarket

when she _____ (run) into Michael.

4. Lisa _____ (wait) in line to vote when

she _____ (meet) Ken.

5. The mailman _____ (deliver) letters when

a dog _____ (bite) him.

E. Form questions with the subject and verb. Answer them. Follow the example.

Example: Where *were the children going* (children/go) when it *started* (start) to rain?

They were going to school.

1. What _____ (bank manager/explain)

to Cindy when his phone _____ (ring)?

_____ .

2. Where _____ (Fred/go) when the

   police _____ (catch) him?

   _____ .

3. What _____ (Michael/do) when the

   lights _____ (go) out?

   _____ .

4. What _____ (Ron/dream) about when

   his alarm clock _____ (ring)?

   _____ .

5. When Cindy _____ (enter) the bank, what

   _____ (teller/do)?

   _____ .

F. Complete these conversations.

   Example: What were you doing when I saw you this morning?

   I was waiting for the bus.

1. Who were you talking to when I saw you?

   _____ to a friend.

2. _____ ?

   I was cashing a check.

3. _____ when the accident happened?

   I was going to class.

4. _____ ?

   I was taking a shower.

5. _____ when the fire started?

   _____ .

G. Combine the two sentences.

Example: Cindy and Ron were walking in the park yesterday. A man tried to take Cindy's purse.

Cindy and Ron were walking in the park yesterday when a man tried to take Cindy's purse.

1. The man was running away with Cindy's purse. Ron tripped him and he dropped the purse.

2. Lisa was driving to the bank. It started to rain.

3. Cindy was filling out a signature card to open a checking account. Her pen ran out of ink.

4. Michael was watching TV last night. His TV broke.

5. Ken and Lisa were living in New York. They fell in love.

H. Complete the questions. Answer them.

1. What were you doing when_____

_____?

_____.

2. Were you going to the bank when_____

_____?

_____.

3. Where were Ron and Cindy walking when_____

_____?

_____.

4. Were you sleeping when _____

_____?

_____.

5. Where were you going when _____

_____?

_____.

I. Fill in the blanks with the correct form of the verb. Use the past tense or past continuous tense.

Cindy _____ (lose) her purse again. She finally _____

(decide) to open a checking account. She _____ (go) to the bank yesterday.

When she _____ (arrive), the bank manager _____ (talk) to

another customer. When the customer left, Cindy _____ (ask) the bank

manager for information about checking accounts. Cindy _____ (fill) out

the signature card when the phone _____ (ring). When the bank manager

finished talking on the phone, Cindy _____ (give) him her paycheck to

deposit in her new account.

   Cindy's checking account _____ (be) free, but she _____

(pay) $3.75 for 200 checks. The bank is going to send her the checks. The checks are going to

have her name, address, and account number on them.

Dialogue

The Consumer Education class is taking a break. The students are talking in the hall. Cindy wants to buy a candy bar from the vending machine.

Cindy:
Oh, no, my purse! Where is it?

Ron:
Not again! Did you leave it in the classroom?

Cindy:
Oh, yeah. Of course. That's where I left it.

(Back in Class)

Cindy:
Michael, can we talk about checking accounts? I want to open one, but I need more information.

Barbara:
You don't have a checking account? How can you live without one? Everyone should have one. They're so convenient. You don't have to pay your bills in person. You just write a check and mail it. It saves gas and time, and it's safe.

Michael:
And your canceled checks are your receipts.

Cindy:
What do you mean "canceled checks"?

Michael:
After you use your checks, the bank sends them back to you at the end of the month. That way, you have a record of the money you spent.

Barbara:
Yesterday I was shopping when I saw a dress that I really liked. It was perfect for work. I didn't have a lot of cash with me, so I wrote a check to pay for it.

Cindy:
Do stores accept checks instead of cash?

Barbara:
Some stores do. But you have to have identification, like a driver's license or a credit card.

Cindy:
Do banks charge for checking accounts?

Barbara:
Mine doesn't. I only have to pay for my checks. I think I pay about $3.50 for 200 checks.

Lisa:
Our bank requires a minimum balance. We have to keep $50 in our account.

Michael:
And some banks have a service charge. For example, you have to pay 10¢ for each check or $2.00 a month. Cindy, you should check several banks to find the best plan for you.

Comprehension Questions

1. Why does Cindy need her purse?

2. Where did she leave it?

3. Why does Barbara like checking accounts?

4. What are "canceled checks"?

5. Why did Barbara use a check yesterday?

6. What do you have to have to use a check in a store?

7. Is there a charge for checking accounts?

8. What are the advantages of a checking account?

Grammar Practice

Must/Have to

Must

Must is followed by the simple form of the verb. *Must* refers to the present or future. *Must* means that it is necessary to do something. It implies an obligation, for example, *You must stop your car at a red light.*

Must not means that it is necessary *not* to do something. It is forbidden. For example, *We must not break the law.*

	Subject	Must	Verb (simple form)	Complement
Affirmative	You	must	sign	a signature card.
Negative	Children	must not mustn't	play	in the street.
Short Answer	Yes, you must.			
	No, you mustn't.			

Have to

Must and *have to* generally express the same meaning in the affirmative, but *have to* is more common in conversations. *Must* occurs in formal speech and writing. *Have to* is usually used instead of *must* to ask a question, for example, *Do I have to work today?*

In the negative, there is a difference in meaning between *must* and *have to. Must not* means that something is forbidden. *Don't have to* means that it is not necessary to do something. It expresses a lack of obligation, for example, *Friday is a holiday; I don't have to go to work.*

Affirmative	Cindy has to open a checking account.
	Ken and Lisa have to save money.
Negative	Children don't have to work.
Question Form	Do I have to go to school today?

Short Answer	Yes, you have to.	No, you don't have to.
	or	*or*
	Yes, you do.	No, you don't.

Must/Have to: Exercises

A. Fill in the blank with *must* and the verb.

Example: Fred, the bank robber, *must go* (go) to jail.

1. Ron and Cindy _____ (tell) the bank their social security numbers to open an account.

2. You _____ (sign) a signature card to open a savings or checking account.

3. Barbara _____ (have) identification to use a check in a store.

4. You _____ (endorse) a check in order to cash it.

5. I _____ (pay) my rent every month.

B. Fill in the blank with *must not* and the verb.

Example: The sign says "No Smoking."

You *must not smoke* (smoke) here.

1. You _____ (stand) under a tree in a storm.

2. You _____ (drive) on the wrong side of the street.

3. Barbara _____ (pay) her bills late.

4. You _____ (use) a pencil to write a check.

5. The sign says "Don't walk." You _____ (cross) the street.

C. Fill in the blanks with *has to* or *doesn't have to*.

Fred, the ex-bank robber, is in prison now. He _____ get up at 6 a.m. every

morning. He _____ wear a gray uniform. He _____ buy

new clothes. He _____ work hard all day. He _____

pay taxes. He _____ pay rent. He _____ buy gas for his

car. At 10 p.m. he _____ go to bed.

D. Form *yes/no* questions with *have to* and the following phrases. Write a short answer in the affirmative or negative.

Example: go to jail

Does Fred have to go to jail?
Yes, he has to.

1. stop at a red light

2. answer the phone

3. pay bills on time

4. get up at 6 a.m.

5. use a pen to write a check

6. obey the law

7. open a checking account

8. be on time

E. Complete these conversations. Use *must* or *have to.*

Example: Ron, *do I have to* open a checking account? I don't need one.

_Yes you do. You always lose your purse._____

1. Mom _____ go to school today?
Yes, you have to.

2. What _____ this afternoon?
I have to do my laundry.

3. Why _____ leave so early?

_____.

4. _____ sign a signature card to open a bank account?

_____.

5. _____ pay her bills in person?

No, _____.

6. _____?
No, you don't have to. You can do it tomorrow.

F. Answer the questions. Use *should, must,* or *have to.*

1. Cindy has a check that she wants to deposit. It says, "Pay to the order of Cynthia S. Hudson." How should she endorse it? ("Endorse" means to sign her name on the back of the check.)

2. The bank sends Barbara her old checks with her bank statement. What should Barbara do with them?

3. Mr. Jones is always late. Today he's starting a new job. What does Mrs. Jones say to him?

4. Ron usually gets up at 5:30 a.m. to go to work. Tomorrow is a holiday. Why is he happy?

5. You're going 75 mph on the highway. A police car is following you with the light flashing. What do you have to do?

G. Give advice, suggestions, or make comments about the following situations. Use *should, have to,* or *must.*

Example: Mr. Jones is very fat.

  Comment: *He should go on a diet.*

1. My friend's car is broken. I know how to fix it.

2. Your apartment is on fire.

3. The gas tank is almost empty.

4. Barbara needs money to buy a car.

5. Your friend's going for an interview for a new job. His hair is dirty, and he's wearing blue jeans.

6. Ron has a toothache.

7. My husband/wife wants to find a new job.

8. Cindy endorsed her check before she arrived at the bank.

9. Barbara's writing a check for $50, but she only has $45 in her checking account.

10. Your friend's writing a check. He's using a pencil.

Dialogue

Barbara is at home. She's opening the mail. Her friend Jane is with her.

Barbara:
Oh, no!

Jane:
What's wrong?

Barbara:
It's a letter from the bank. My check bounced and I have to pay $6.

Jane:
How did that happen?

Barbara:
I wrote a check for $28.99 to pay for a dress, but I only had $19.24 in my checking account.

Jane:
Didn't you deposit your paycheck?

Barbara:
No, I forgot to. I have to be more careful next time.

Comprehension Questions

1. Why did Barbara's check bounce?

2. Why didn't Barbara deposit her paycheck?

3. How much did the bank charge Barbara? Why is there a charge?

Reading

Applying for a Credit Card

Barbara went to the bank three weeks ago. She deposited money in her checking account. She decided to apply for a credit card. Barbara can use it in many clothing stores, restaurants, hotels, gas stations, etc. She can use it instead of cash. Barbara filled out an application.

Here is an example of a credit card application:

INFORMATION ABOUT APPLICANT

Last Name	First Name	Middle Name	Birthdate	Telephone Number ( )
Present Street Address		Apt. No.	At Present Address ____Yrs. ____Mos.	☐ Rent ☐ Buying ☐ Live w/Parents
City State		Zip Code	Social Security No.	Education ☐ High School ☐ Part College ☐ College Degree ☐ Graduate Degree
Previous Address		Apt. No.	At Previous Address ____Yrs. Mos.	
City State		Zip Code	Driver's License No.	Dependents No.____ Ages____
Name and Address of Nearest Relative Not Living With You			Relationship	Telephone Number ( )
Present Employer			Position (If Self-Employed Give Nature of Business) ____Yrs. ____Mos.	
Street Address			Business Telephone	Monthly Job Income
City State		Zip Code	Previous Employer	
Previous Employer Address			Position ____Yrs. ____Mos.	
Source of other income, if any: (Alimony, child support, or separate maintenance income need not be revealed if you do not wish to have it considered as a basis for repaying this obligation.)				Monthly Amount

ASSET AND DEBT INFORMATION

Autos Owned (State whose name registered)	License No.	Make/Model/Year	Value
Cash Value Life Insurance		Issuer	Face Value
Real Estate and Location		Date Acquired	Value

Checking Accounts		Savings Accounts	
Bank Branch		Bank Branch	
Acct. No.	Balance	Acct. No.	Balance

List banks, department stores, finance companies (including alimony/child support obligations)

Name of Creditor	Branch or Location	Account Number	Balance	Mo. Pymt.

Last week Barbara received her credit card. Yesterday she used it for the first time. She bought a dress for $32.95. She paid for it with her credit card. This is how: She gave her credit card to the clerk. The clerk filled out a charge form. Barbara signed the form. It had three copies. One copy was for Barbara, one copy was for the store, and one copy was for the bank.

After Barbara signed the charge form, the clerk gave her a copy. Barbara should keep her copy because it's a record of her purchase.

Here is the charge form:

626 23123 123 110	5397872

Barbara Graham

Date 3-2-91	Authorization	Clerk 2	Dept.	Identification	Take ✓
					Send

Quan.	Class	Description		Price	Amount	
1		Dress			32	95

Currency	Date	Amount	Sub Tot.	
Cardholder Sign Here			Tax	
Barbara Graham			Total	32	95

BANKCARD SLIP
CUSTOMER COPY

THE FASHION SHOP
PITTSBURGH, PA 15257

IMPORTANT: RETAIN THIS COPY FOR YOUR RECORDS

Once a month Barbara receives a bill in the mail from the credit card company. It lists the stores where she used her credit card and the amounts she charged during that month.

Here is the bill she received for the dress purchase:

IMPORTANT: Please Retain This Portion Of Your Statement, It Is Your Permanent Record. Payment Of Any Amounts In Dispute Is Not Required Pending Resolution.   To Report Lost Or Stolen Card Telephone (314) 425-8060

DATE	REFERENCE NUMBER	DESCRIPTION	PURCHASES	PAYMENTS OR CREDITS
3-2-91	15080050536	The Fashion Shop	32.95	
			TO PAY IN FULL PAY THIS AMOUNT ⬇	TO MAKE MINIMUM PAYMENT PAY THIS AMOUNT ⬇

Previous Balance	Payments	Credits	Finance Charge	Purchases	Cash Advance	Credit Life Premium	New Balance	Minimum Payment Due
				32.95			32.95	10.00

Closing Date	Your Account Number	Computed On Average Daily Balance Of	Annual Percentage Rate	Your Credit Limit	To Avoid Additional Finance Chrages Pay New Balance By	You Have Unused Credit Of
3-13-91	626 23123 123 110			500.00	4-10-91	467.05

She should pay the bill within 30 days of the billing date. If she doesn't pay the bill in 30 days, she must pay 1¼% interest each month or 15% interest a year.

Barbara uses her credit card because it's convenient. With her credit card she can buy things now and pay for them later. But Barbara must be careful. Some people use credit cards too much. At the end of the month, they receive their bills and they don't have enough money to pay them. Then they must pay a high interest. Barbara must remember to buy only what she needs and what she can afford.

Comprehension Questions

Write the answers to the following questions.

1. Why did Barbara go to the bank three weeks ago?

2. What is a credit card?

3. Where can Barbara use it?

4. What information did Barbara have to fill out on the application?

5. How long did it take for Barbara to receive her credit card?

6. What did Barbara buy with her credit card? How much was it?

7. What information is on the charge form?

8. Why should Barbara keep her copy of the charge form?

9. How often does Barbara receive her credit card bill?

10. What information is on the bill?

11. Why should Barbara pay the bill within 30 days of the billing date?

12. Why does Barbara use her credit card?

13. Why does Barbara have to be careful when she buys on credit?

Listening Comprehension

A. Circle the number that your teacher says.

1. Barbara's address is (1727, 7027) Walnut Street.

2. Mr. Jones completed the application for a new job in (13, 30) minutes.

3. Ken paid ($15.37, $50.37) for a new pair of shoes.

4. Barbara was (14, 40) minutes late for class last night.

5. Michael bought three books last week. They cost ($16.95, $60.95).

6. Ron spent (19, 90) minutes fixing a car.

7. Ron has ($18, $80) in his pocket.

8. Lisa withdrew ($13.50, $30.50) from her savings account.

9. Ken and Lisa live at (1463, 4063) Highland Avenue.

10. Tomatoes cost (15¢, 50¢) a pound today in the supermarket.

B. Fill in the blanks with the number that your teacher says. Remember to use the dollar sign and the decimal point.

Barbara has to pay the following bills this month. Her electric bill is _____. Her gas bill

is _____. Her water bill is _____. Her telephone bill this month is _____. Barbara

went to the doctor. She pays him _____ a month. Barbara's rent is _____ a month. She

bought a new dress. She used her credit card. The dress cost _____.

Problem Solving

Checking

A. Yesterday Barbara paid her bills. Look at the check she wrote for her electric bill. She must write checks with a *pen,* not a pencil.

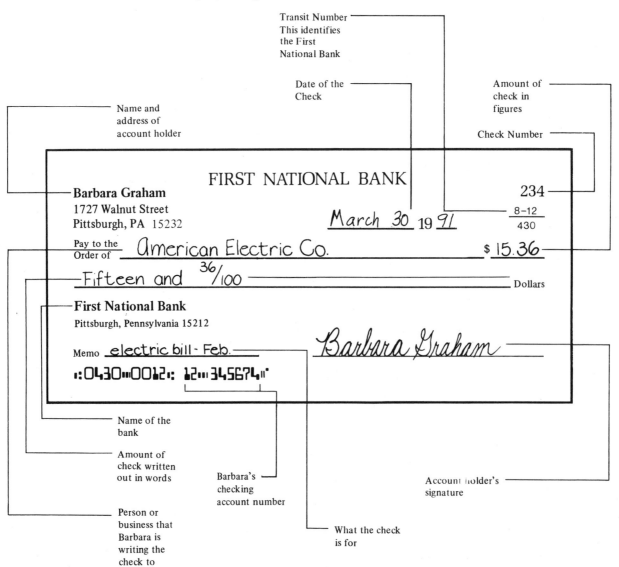

Write a check for Barbara to pay her gas bill:

Columbia Gas Co. $13.21

```
┌──────────────────────────────────────────────────────────────┐
│                    FIRST NATIONAL BANK              235        │
│ Barbara Graham                                                 │
│ 1727 Walnut Street                                      8–12   │
│ Pittsburgh, PA 15232              _____ 19 __        ────   │
│                                                         430    │
│ Pay to the                                          $          │
│ Order of _____            │
│                                                               │
│ _____ Dollars       │
│                                                               │
│ First National Bank                                           │
│ Pittsburgh, Pennsylvania 15212                                │
│                                                               │
│ Memo _____    _____           │
│  ⑊:0430⑊0012⑊: 12⑊345674⑊                                     │
└──────────────────────────────────────────────────────────────┘
```

Now write out each amount that Barbara must pay for her bills.

1. Check #234: American Electric Co. $15.36

2. Check #235: Columbia Gas Co. $13.21

3. Check #236: City Water Co. $9.45

4. Check #237: People's Telephone Co. $19.64

5. Check #238: Dr. Lee Morrison $11.50

6. Check #239: Acme Realty Co. $304.00

_____

7. Check #240: MasterCard $32.95

_____

B. Balance Barbara's checkbook. Enter each check and then deduct the amount from the balance. What is her balance after she pays her bills?

PLEASE BE SURE TO **DEDUCT** ANY PER CHECK CHARGES OR SERVICE CHARGES THAT MAY APPLY TO YOUR ACCOUNT

CHECK NO.	DATE	CHECKS ISSUED TO OR DESCRIPTION OF DEPOSIT	(−) AMOUNT OF CHECK		√ T	(−) CHECK FEE (IF ANY)	(+) AMOUNT OF DEPOSIT	BALANCE $ 15	06
	3/16/91	Deposit					382	96	382	96
								398	02
234	3/16/91	American Electric Co.	$15	36				15	36
								382	66

REMEMBER TO RECORD AUTOMATIC PAYMENTS / DEPOSITS ON DATE AUTHORIZED.

C. At the end of the month Barbara's going to receive a bank statement in the mail from First National Bank. Her bank statement tells her how much money she has in her account. Check her bank statement with her checkbook. Did the bank pay all her checks? Barbara's canceled checks are her receipts. What should she do with them? According to the bank Barbara has $103.41 in her account. If she writes a check for $104 the check will *bounce.* The bank charges her a service charge if one of her checks bounces.

FIRST NATIONAL BANK
of PITTSBURGH

3—30—91	4—30—91	12345674
Date Last Statement	Statement Date	Account Number

Ms. Barbara Graham
1727 Walnut Street
Pittsburgh, PA 15232

Balance From Last Statement	No. Chcks	Amount of Checks Paid This Period	No. Dpsts	Amount of Deposits This Period	Closing Balance
115 06	6	294 61	1 -	382 96	103 41

Date	Checks and Other Debits	Deposits and Credits	Balance
3 16		382 96	498 02
3 30	15 36		482 66
3 30	13 21		469 45
3 30	9 45		460 00
3 30	19 64		440 36
3 30	304 00		136 36
3 30	32 95		103 41

D. Barbara deposited her paycheck in her checking account on March 16. She endorsed it at the bank. She did not endorse it before she arrived. This is how she endorsed it.

SUNSHINE TRAVEL $\frac{5-9}{420}$
435 E. 6TH ST., PITTSBURGH, PA 15112

PAYROLL CHECK 225012

Date		
3	13	91

Pay
To The
Order
Of

Barbara S. Graham
1727 Walnut Street
Pittsburgh, PA 15232

Amount
$ 382 96

James C. Roberts
Charles R. South

Fidelity Bank
Pittsburgh, PA

⑊225003⑊ ⑊0143⑊0079⑊ 633⑊5647⑊

FOR DEPOSIT ONLY
Barbara S. Graham

She must endorse the check exactly the way it's paid to her. If Barbara wants to cash her check, she doesn't write "For Deposit Only." She writes only her name.

Barbara filled out a deposit slip to deposit her check. Here is a sample of the deposit slip. Fill it out for Barbara.

CHECKING ACCOUNT DEPOSIT TICKET	CASH			
	LIST CHECKS SINGLY			
Barbara Graham				
1727 Walnut Street				8-12
Pittsburgh, PA 15232				430
				USE OTHER SIDE FOR ADDITIONAL LISTING
DATE _____ 19 ___	TOTAL FROM OTHER SIDE			♦ ENTER TOTAL HERE
CHECKS AND OTHER ITEMS ARE RECEIVED FOR DEPOSIT SUBJECT TO THE PROVISIONS OF THE UNIFORM COMMERCIAL CODE OR ANY APPLICABLE COLLECTION AGREEMENT	TOTAL			BE SURE EACH ITEM IS PROPERLY ENDORSED
DEPOSITED IN				
First National Bank				
Pittsburgh, Pennsylvania 15212				

⑃:0430⑉0012⑉: 12⑉345674⑈

DE LUXE HD - 4

CHECKS LIST SINGLY	DOLLARS	CENTS
1		
2		
3		
4		
5		
6		
7		
8		
9		
10		
11		
12		
13		
14		
15		
16		
17		
18		
19		
TOTAL		
ENTER TOTAL ON THE FRONT OF THIS TICKET		

Unit Four

 # Supermarkets

Learner Objectives

Consumer Competencies

Being able to prepare a shopping list and to list the items according to the departments in a supermarket

Developing an understanding of some of the basic rules to follow when shopping in a supermarket

Being able to recognize and use the names and abbreviations of containers, units, and measures

Understanding how items are grouped in a supermarket and where to find them

Becoming familiar with the information on a food label

Being able to understand the basic ideas of unit pricing and to do some computation on unit pricing

Grammatical Structures

Being able to understand and use the following structures: countable/noncountable nouns with *some/any, much/many, a little/a few/a lot of*; prepositions of location; and indirect questions

Vocabulary Items

Being able to understand and use the following words in context:

Nouns	ingredient	volume
abbreviation	item	
aisle	label	*Verbs*
baking needs	measure	advertise
bargain	net weight	check out
brand	nutritional	put away
container	information	
dairy products	produce	*Adjectives*
department	product	crowded
express lane	shelf	on sale
fight	specials	
frozen food	staples	
grocery	unit	
household cleaners	unit price	

Dialogue

Ken went to the supermarket. He is home now. He and Lisa are putting away the groceries. They are having an argument.

Lisa:
Ken, why did you buy steak? How much was it?

Ken:
$3.50 a pound.

Lisa:
$3.50 a pound! I wrote *two pounds of hamburger* on the list. Why didn't you buy hamburger?

Ken:
Because I like steak.

Lisa:
Ken, we made a budget. We can't buy steak every week on our budget. It's expensive. We spend too much money on food.

Ken:
I know, but I'm tired of hamburger!

Lisa:
A *small* box of laundry detergent! The small box is expensive. I wrote *20 pounds of laundry detergent* on the list.

Ken:
What list?

Lisa:
The shopping list. I gave it to you before you went to the supermarket.

Ken:
I don't like to use a list. I buy what we need and what I want.

Lisa:
When we use a list, we buy only what we need. We save money that way.

Ken:
Lists aren't important. They're not necessary.

Lisa:
Well, I think they are. Let's ask Michael, our Consumer Education teacher, about this.

Comprehension Questions

1. Where did Ken go?

2. What are he and Lisa doing now?

3. What did Ken buy? How much did it cost?

4. What did Lisa write on the list?

5. Why did Ken buy steak? Why should he buy hamburger instead of steak?

6. What size box of laundry detergent did Ken buy?

7. Did Ken use the list? Why not? How does Ken shop?

8. Why does Lisa think that they should use a list?

9. What are they going to ask Michael?

Grammar Practice

Some/Any

We use the words *some* and *any* to indicate an indefinite quantity. We use both *some* and *any* in questions although *any* is more common. We use *some* in affirmative statements and *any* in negative statements.

Question form	Do we have *any* potatoes?
	Do we have *some* potatoes?
Affirmative	Yes, we have *some* potatoes.
Negative	No, we don't have *any* potatoes.
Short answer	Yes, we have *some*.
	Yes, we do.
	No, we don't have *any*.
	No, we don't.

Some/Any: **Exercises**

A. Ken went to the supermarket this morning. Lisa wants to make lunch now, but she needs to know what Ken bought. To find out what Ken bought, form questions and answers using the following items with *some* or *any*.

Example: bread

Lisa: *Did you buy any bread?*

Ken: Yes, *I bought some bread.*
              or
        Yes, *I bought some.*
              or
        Yes, *I did.*

1. milk

   Lisa:

   Ken: Yes,

2. soup

   Lisa:

   Ken: No,

3. crackers

   Lisa:

   Ken: No,

4. peanut butter

   Lisa:

   Ken: Yes,

5. jelly

   Lisa:

   Ken: Yes,

6. ham

   Lisa:

   Ken: Yes,

7. mustard

Lisa:

Ken: No,

8. cheese

Lisa:

Ken: No,

9. Coke

Lisa:

Ken: Yes,

10. potato chips

Lisa:

Ken: No,

B. Make sentences with *didn't have any* and *needed some* for these situations.

Example: Situation:
Lisa ate the last piece of bread. Ken wanted to make a sandwich.

Ken *didn't have any* bread.
He *needed some* bread.

1. Ken used the last egg for breakfast. Lisa wanted to bake a cake.

2. Fred, the ex-bank robber, wanted to buy a new car, but the police took all his money.

3. Cindy and Ron wanted to drive to the mountains, but the gas tank was empty.

4. Mr. and Mrs. Jones ate an excellent dinner at a restaurant. Mr. Jones wanted to pay the bill, but his wallet was empty.

5. Lisa used all the shampoo. Ken wanted to wash his hair.

Reading

In their Consumer Education class, Lisa and Ken read the following information about supermarket shopping.

Before you go to the supermarket, you should check to see what you have at home. Look in your refrigerator and freezer. Be sure to check your staples—flour, sugar, salt, bread, etc. Then you should make a list of what you need. Organize the list according to the departments in the supermarket. For example, list all the dairy products—milk, eggs, butter, etc.—together.

At the supermarket, you should buy only what you need and what you can use. Supermarkets advertise a lot and offer "specials" because they want you to buy a lot. Be careful. And remember these important points: Don't shop when you're hungry, tired, or in a hurry, and don't shop when the stores are crowded.

Comprehension Questions

Write the answers to the following questions.

1. What should you do before you go to the supermarket?

2. What are staples?

3. How should you organize your shopping list?

4. Should you buy all the specials at the supermarket? Why or why not?

5. When shouldn't you go to the supermarket? Why?

6. Why should you be careful when you shop at a supermarket?

7. Should you be careful when you shop at other stores? Why?

Grammar Practice

Countable/Noncountable Nouns

Countable Nouns

We can count some nouns, for example, *apples, bananas, children.* These are countable nouns. Countable nouns can take an indefinite article in the singular, and they have plural forms.

We can say:

a banana	a child
one banana	one child
ten bananas	ten children
some bananas	some children

Noncountable Nouns

We cannot count some nouns in their original mass form, for example, *milk, water, oil.* These are noncountable nouns. Noncountable nouns cannot take an indefinite article and do not have a plural form. We do not use *a, one, two,* etc. before them. We use the singular form of the verb with them.

We say:
milk
some milk

Some nouns may be countable or noncountable, depending on their meaning. For example:

The *food* was delicious. (noncountable)

Convenience *foods* are popular with busy people. (countable)

Countable/Noncountable Nouns: Exercises

A. Here is a list of the names of the items in the pictures. Write the name of each item next to its picture. Are these items countable or noncountable?

sugar	rice	butter
cereal	carrot	milk
meat	cheese	flour
onion	tomato	laundry detergent
soap	bread	salt
oil	banana	soup
coffee	egg	

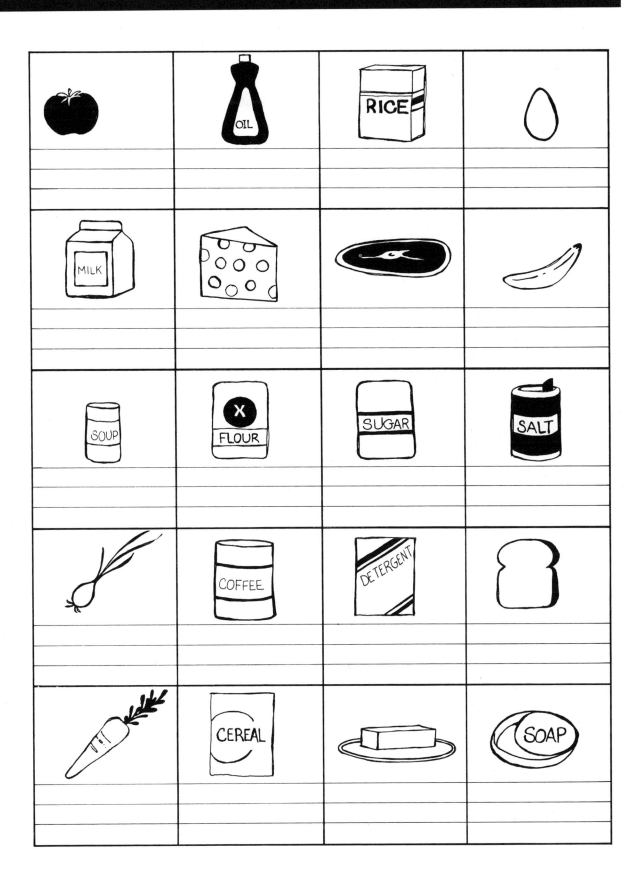

B. To count noncountable nouns, we put a unit of measure and *of* before them, for example:

a *bottle* of milk

three *slices* of cheese

five *pounds* of flour

We can also use these names of containers (a bottle), units (three slices), and measures (five pounds) with countable nouns. Here is a list of containers, units, and measures.

Containers

bag (of potatoes, apples, sugar, flour, rice, potato chips)

bottle (of ketchup, wine, oil, soda, beer)

box (of laundry detergent, cereal, crackers, salt, rice)

can (of soup, soda, coffee, vegetables, tuna, tomato sauce)

carton (of milk, eggs, ice cream)

jar (of mustard, peanut butter, mayonnaise, olives, pickles)

pack (of cigarettes, gum)

package (of cheese, napkins, hot dogs)

Units

bar (of soap)

bunch (of bananas, grapes, carrots, celery)

cup (of flour, sugar)

dozen/half a dozen (donuts, eggs, cookies)   NOTE: We do not use *of* after *dozen*.

head (of lettuce)

loaf (of bread); *plural* - loaves of bread

piece (of cake, candy, bubble gum, fish)

slice (of cheese, bacon, bread, meat, ham)

Measures

Abbreviations*	Liquid	Dry
ounce = oz.	8 fl. oz. = 1 cup	16 oz. = 1 lb.
fluid ounce = fl. oz.	2 cups = 1 pt.	8 oz. = 1 cup
pound = lb.	16 oz. = 1 pt.	
pint = pt.	4 cups = 1 qt.	
quart = qt.	2 pt. = 1 qt.	
gallon = gal.	32 oz. = 1 qt.	
dozen = doz.	4 qt. = 1 gal.	
	128 oz. = 1 gal.	

*Abbreviations are the same in the singular and plural.

Metric

Dry	Liquid
1 oz. = 28 grams	1 fl. oz. = .03 liter
3.5 oz. = 100 grams	1 qt. = .95 liter
1 lb. = .45 kilograms	1 gallon = 3.79 liters
2.2 lb. = 1 kilogram	33.8 fl. oz. = 1 liter

Look at the pictures of the items again. Write the names of containers, units, and measures that we can use with each item.

Much/Many

We use the word *much* with noncountable nouns and *many* with countable nouns. To ask about quantity we say *How much* or *How many,* for example,

How many apples do you need?
How much cheese do you need?

Much/Many: **Exercises**

A. Look at the pictures of the items again. Decide if each of the items is countable or noncountable. Write the word *many* next to the countable items and *much* next to the noncountable items.

B. Ron and Cindy are planning a dinner party for eight people. They are making a shopping list. Fill in the blanks with *How much* or *How many.*

Example: Ron: *How much* rice should we buy?

Cindy: One box.

1. Ron: _____ meat should we buy?
    Cindy: Four pounds.

2. Ron: _____ lettuce should we buy?
    Cindy: Two heads.

3. Ron: _____ tomatoes should we buy?
    Cindy: Two pounds.

4. Ron: _____ cucumbers should we buy?
    Cindy: Three.

5. Ron: _____ wine should we buy?
    Cindy: Four bottles.

Continue this conversation between Cindy and Ron. Make questions with *How much* or *How many*. Answer the questions with the name of a container, a unit, or a measure.

6. onions

7. coffee

8. milk

9. butter

10. carrots

11. bread

12. salad dressing

13. fruit

14. napkins

15. ice cream

A Little/A Few/A Lot Of

We use the words *a little* with noncountable nouns and *a few* with countable nouns to indicate a small quantity. *A lot* indicates a large quantity. We use *a lot of* with both countable and noncountable nouns.

Countable Nouns

Question form	Do you want a lot of apples?
Affirmative	I want a lot of apples.
	I want a few apples.
Negative	I don't want a lot of apples.
Short answer	Yes, I want a lot. *or* Yes, I do.
	No, I want a few. *or* No, I don't.

Noncountable Nouns

Question form	Do you want a lot of rice?
Affirmative	I want a lot of rice. I want a little rice.
Negative	I don't want a lot of rice.
Short answer	Yes, I want a lot. *or* Yes, I do. No, I want a little. *or* No, I don't.

A Little/A Few/A Lot Of: **Exercises**

A. Look at the pictures of the items again. Write *a little* next to noncountable items and *a few* next to countable items.

B. Write the opposite. Use *a little* or *a few.*

Example: I want *a lot of* bread.
Opposite: *I want a little bread.* _____

1. I cooked a lot of bacon.

   _____.

2. I drank a lot of milk.

   _____.

3. I need a lot of money.

   _____.

4. I chewed a lot of gum.

   _____.

5. I ate a lot of ice cream.

   _____.

6. I ate a lot of peanuts.

   _____.

7. I bought a lot of fruit.

   _____.

8. I ate a lot of sandwiches.

9. I want a lot of potato chips.

10. I drank a lot of orange juice.

C. Make questions in the past tense with the item, the verb, and *a lot of.* Answer the questions with *only a few* or *only a little.*

Example: buy/spinach

Did you buy a lot of spinach?
No, only a little.

1. buy/toothpaste

2. drink/coffee

3. eat/bread

4. eat/chicken

5. cook/fish

6. buy/cereal

7. eat/strawberries

8. drink/milk

9. buy/lemons

10. cook/potatoes

D. Make questions with *How much* or *How many.* Answer with *Only a few* or *Only a little.*

Example: Barbara doesn't like eggs. She eats only three eggs a month.

How many eggs does Barbara eat?
Only a few.

1. Ken bought five pounds of laundry detergent at the supermarket last week. Lisa usually buys twenty pounds.

2. Ron's home only about two evenings a week. The other evenings he's with Cindy.

3. Mr. Jones loves cake, but he eats only two pieces of cake a week because he's overweight.

4. The foreign student knows some English, but only words like "Hello" and "How are you?"

5. Ron and Cindy went shopping downtown only two or three times last month.

6. Michael doesn't like fish very much. He eats fish only about once a week.

7. Mr. and Mrs. Jones used only two or three pounds of coffee last year.

8. Mrs. Jones spends $20 a week on groceries.

9. Last week Ron had dinner at home only three times.

10. Last year Mr. Jones drank whiskey only at Christmas, and then he drank only one glass.

E. Barbara's checking to see what she needs at the supermarket. Her friend Jane is helping her. Jane's making a list of the items that Barbara needs.

Jane:	Do you have any milk?
Barbara:	*Only a little.*
Jane:	*How much* milk do you need?
Barbara:	I need *one carton.*

Follow the pattern. Answer the first question with *Only a little* or *Only a few.* Answer the question *How much* or *How many* with the name of a container, a unit, or a measure.

1. Jane: Do you have any rice?

   Barbara: _____.

   Jane: _____ rice do you need?

   Barbara: I need_____.

2. Jane: Do you have any peanut butter?

   Barbara: _____.

   Jane: _____ peanut butter do you need?

   Barbara: I need_____.

3. Jane: Do you have any cheese?

Barbara: _____.

Jane: _____ cheese do you need?

Barbara: I need_____.

4. Jane: Do you have any soup?

Barbara: _____.

Jane: _____ soup do you need?

Barbara: I need_____.

5. Jane: Do you have any coffee?

Barbara: _____.

Jane: _____ coffee do you need?

Barbara: I need_____.

6. Jane: Do you have any cereal?

Barbara: _____.

Jane: _____ cereal do you need?

Barbara: I need_____.

7. Jane: Do you have any bread?

Barbara: _____.

Jane: _____ bread do you need?

Barbara: I need_____.

8. Jane: Do you have any orange juice?

Barbara: _____.

Jane: _____ orange juice do you need?

Barbara: I need_____.

Problem Solving

Barbara needs to buy the following items at the supermarket.

milk	bananas	bread	fresh mushrooms
rice	cheese	hamburger	laundry detergent
soup	coffee	cereal	frozen orange juice
sugar	napkins	peanut butter	tomato sauce

Make a shopping list for Barbara. Here are the departments in the supermarket. Write each item under the department where Barbara can find it.

Dairy Products

Baking Needs

Produce

Other Grocery Items
(including salad dressing, mustard, peanut butter, coffee, tea, rice, pasta)

Canned Vegetables
(including soup, tuna, tomato sauce)

Cereal

Bread

Household Cleaners

Frozen Foods

Paper Products

Meat

Summary

Countable/Noncountable Nouns

Countable Nouns

Questions

Do you need any lemons?

Do you need some lemons?

How many lemons do you want?

Affirmative

I need a lemon.

I need two lemons.

I want some lemons.

I want a few lemons.

I need a lot of lemons.

Negative

I don't need any lemons.

Noncountable Nouns

Questions

Do you need any rice?

Do you need some rice?

How much rice do you want?

Affirmative

I need rice.

I want some rice.

I want a little rice.

I need a lot of rice.

Negative

I don't need any rice.

Grammar Practice

Prepositions of Location: *in, on, next to, between*

Prepositions of Location: Exercise

Imagine that you work in a supermarket. The customers ask you many questions about where different items are. Answer the questions according to the diagram below of Aisle 4 in the supermarket. Use this pattern:

Customer: Excuse me, can you tell me where the cake mixes are?

You: *Yes, they're in Aisle 4, on the bottom shelf, between the baking soda and the oil.*

1. Excuse me, can you tell me where the white flour is?

   Yes, it's in _____ next to _____

   on _____ .

2. Excuse me, can you tell me where the oil is?

3. Excuse me, can you tell me where the raisins are?

4. Excuse me, can you tell me where the spices are?

5. Excuse me, can you tell me where the sugar is?

6. Excuse me, can you tell me where the chocolate is?

7. Excuse me, can you tell me where the salt is?

8. Excuse me, can you tell me where the whole wheat flour is?

9. Excuse me, can you tell me where the baking soda is?

10. Excuse me, can you tell me where the nuts are?

Dialogue

Lisa went shopping today. She and Ken are putting away the groceries.

Ken:
Look at all these tomatoes! How many pounds did you buy?

Lisa:
Six.

Ken:
Six! Lisa, you know I don't like tomatoes. I never eat them. Why did you buy so many?

Lisa:
Because they were on sale, three pounds for a dollar.

Ken:

What are we going to do with all these tomatoes?

Lisa:

I don't know. But, look, I bought chicken. It was on sale, $.59 a pound.

Ken:

That's good. We can have chicken for dinner this week. Lisa, I think we should buy only the specials when we're going to use the food.

Lisa:

I know. You're right, Ken. But I can't pass up a bargain!

Comprehension Questions

1. Why did Lisa buy so many tomatoes?

2. Why shouldn't she buy a lot of tomatoes?

3. Why did Lisa buy chicken?

4. When should you buy the specials?

Grammar Practice

Indirect Questions

In the supermarket, to find out where something is and how much it costs, we ask:

Excuse me, where is the peanut butter?

Excuse me, how much does this jar of peanut butter cost?

However, sometimes we want to be more polite, so we use the introductory phrases *Can you tell me* and *Do you know* before the questions. We say:

Excuse me, can you tell me where the peanut butter is?

Excuse me, do you know where the peanut butter is?

Excuse me, can you tell me how much this jar of peanut butter costs?

Excuse me, do you know how much this jar of peanut butter costs?

Indirect Questions: Exercises

A. You are at a new supermarket. You need to know where some of the items on your shopping list are. Form polite questions with *Can you tell me* and *Do you know* to ask the location of the items. Answer the questions according to the map on the next page.

Example: 1 dozen oranges

Excuse me, can you tell me where the oranges are?
Yes, they're in the produce department.

Shopping List

5 lb. of sugar

2 cans of peaches

1 can of tuna

2 qt. of 7-Up

1 bag of oatmeal cookies

1 can of coffee

10 lb. of laundry detergent

½ gallon of ice cream

1 lb. of frozen fish

1 lb. of onions

2 loaves of bread

1 lb. of margarine

1 package of hot dogs

1 carton of cottage cheese

1 lb. of fresh mushrooms

1 doz. eggs

3 containers of yogurt

3 cans of frozen orange juice

5 lb. of chuck roast

1 jar of peanut butter

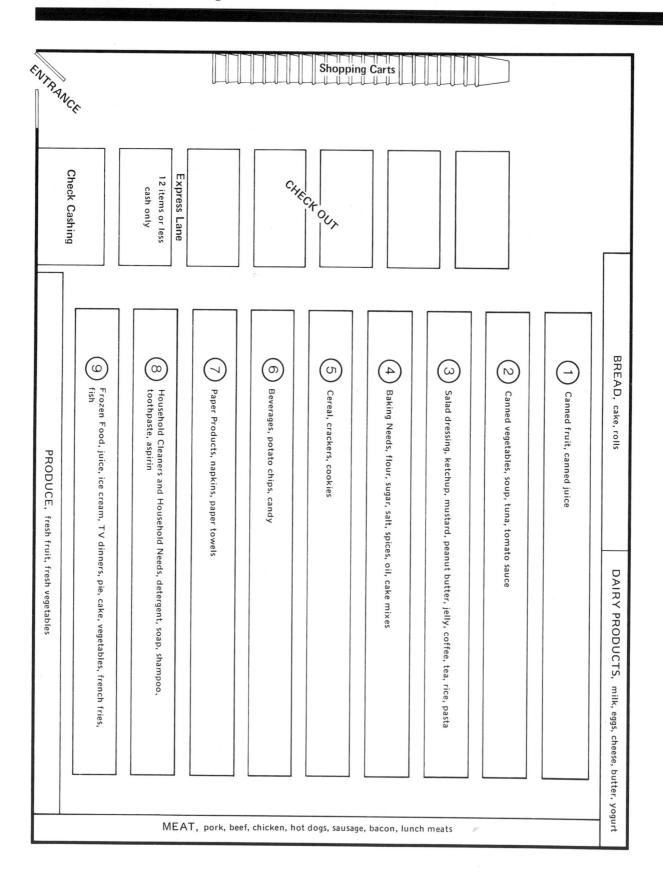

Shopping Carts

ENTRANCE

Check Cashing

Express Lane
12 items or less
cash only

CHECK OUT

BREAD, cake, rolls

DAIRY PRODUCTS, milk, eggs, cheese, butter, yogurt

① Canned fruit, canned juice

② Canned vegetables, soup, tuna, tomato sauce

③ Salad dressing, ketchup, mustard, peanut butter, jelly, coffee, tea, rice, pasta

④ Baking Needs, flour, sugar, salt, spices, oil, cake mixes

⑤ Cereal, crackers, cookies

⑥ Beverages, potato chips, candy

⑦ Paper Products, napkins, paper towels

⑧ Household Cleaners and Household Needs, detergent, soap, shampoo, toothpaste, aspirin

⑨ Frozen Food, juice, ice cream, TV dinners, pie, cake, vegetables, french fries, fish

PRODUCE, fresh fruit, fresh vegetables

MEAT, pork, beef, chicken, hot dogs, sausage, bacon, lunch meats

B. There is no price on some of the items that you want to buy. You want to know the price. Form polite questions with *Can you tell me* and *Do you know* to ask the price of the following items. Use *this* and *these.* Answer the questions.

Example: rice   (59¢/box)

Excuse me, can you tell me how much this rice is?

Yes, it's 59¢ a box.

1. potato chips   (99¢/bag)

2. milk   (95¢/½ gallon)

3. lettuce   (59¢/head)

4. cereal   ($1.29/box)

5. peanut butter   ($1.39/jar)

6. yogurt   (45¢/container)

7. hamburger   ($1.99/lb.)

8. sliced ham   ($1.45/package)

9. frozen cauliflower   (59¢/box)

10. mustard   (89¢/jar)

Reading

Labels

You should learn to read and understand labels. A label has a lot of information that you need to determine the best quality and the best price. Look at this food label. It has the following information.

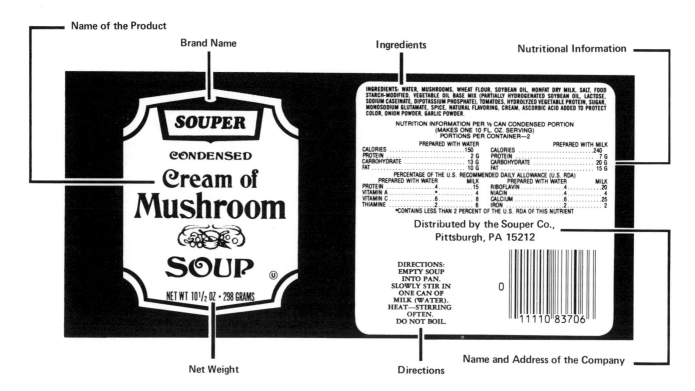

Name of the Product

Brand Name

Ingredients

Nutritional Information

SOUPER

CONDENSED

Cream of **Mushroom** SOUP

NET WT 10½ OZ • 298 GRAMS

INGREDIENTS: WATER, MUSHROOMS, WHEAT FLOUR, SOYBEAN OIL, NONFAT DRY MILK, SALT, FOOD STARCH-MODIFIED, VEGETABLE OIL BASE MIX (PARTIALLY HYDROGENATED SOYBEAN OIL, LACTOSE, SODIUM CASEINATE, DIPOTASSIUM PHOSPHATE), TOMATOES, HYDROLYZED VEGETABLE PROTEIN, SUGAR, MONOSODIUM GLUTAMATE, SPICE, NATURAL FLAVORING, CREAM, ASCORBIC ACID ADDED TO PROTECT COLOR, ONION POWDER, GARLIC POWDER.

NUTRITION INFORMATION PER ½ CAN CONDENSED PORTION
(MAKES ONE 10 FL. OZ. SERVING)
PORTIONS PER CONTAINER—2

	PREPARED WITH WATER		PREPARED WITH MILK
CALORIES	150	CALORIES	240
PROTEIN	2 G	PROTEIN	7 G
CARBOHYDRATE	13 G	CARBOHYDRATE	20 G
FAT	10 G	FAT	15 G

PERCENTAGE OF THE U.S. RECOMMENDED DAILY ALLOWANCE (U.S. RDA)

	PREPARED WITH WATER	MILK		PREPARED WITH WATER	MILK
PROTEIN	4	15	RIBOFLAVIN	4	20
VITAMIN A	*	4	NIACIN	4	4
VITAMIN C	6	8	CALCIUM	6	25
THIAMINE	2	6	IRON	2	2

*CONTAINS LESS THAN 2 PERCENT OF THE U.S. RDA OF THIS NUTRIENT

Distributed by the Souper Co.,
Pittsburgh, PA 15212

DIRECTIONS:
EMPTY SOUP
INTO PAN.
SLOWLY STIR IN
ONE CAN OF
MILK (WATER).
HEAT—STIRRING
OFTEN.
DO NOT BOIL.

0 11110 83706

Net Weight

Directions

Name and Address of the Company

Name of the Product, Brand Name, and Company Name and Address

The name of the product, the brand name, and the name and address of the company that made the product must be on the label.

Net Weight (net wt.)

The net weight must be on the label. It tells you the weight of the food without the container.

Directions

The directions tell you the best way to prepare the product.

Ingredients

The label tells you the items that the product contains. These items are the ingredients. The ingredients are in order of quantity. The main ingredient is first. The label of this product tells you that the soup contains more water than any other ingredient.

Nutritional Information

The label tells you the number of servings in the container, the number of calories per serving, and the amount of protein, carbohydrates, and fat per serving. The label also tells you the percentage of a person's daily food needs that the product supplies.

Date

In many states, milk must have a date on it. The date tells you the last day the product should be sold. The label says "sell by" or "not to be sold after" and the date. Sometimes other items such as dairy products, bread, and meat also have a date on them.

Comprehension Questions

Write the answers to the following questions.

1. Why should you learn to read and understand labels?

2. What information is on a label?

3. What is the net weight?

4. In what order does the label list the ingredients?

5. What nutritional information does the label contain?

6. What does the date on milk tell you?

Unit Pricing

When you are shopping in the supermarket, you should compare prices. To determine the best price, first compare the net weights. If the net weights of the two items are the same, compare the prices to determine the cheapest.

If the net weights are not the same, you have to find out the unit price. The unit price is the price of an item per unit measure, for example, one ounce, one quart, one pound. Some supermarkets give you this information. They tell you the name of the item, weight, unit price, and the price that you pay. If the supermarket doesn't have unit pricing, you can determine it. To determine the unit price, divide the price of the item by the net weight or volume. For example:

The 16-fl.-oz. (1 pt.) bottle of vegetable oil costs 95¢.
The 38-fl.-oz. (1 qt. 6 oz.) bottle costs $2.09, and the 48-fl.-oz. (1 qt. 1 pt.) bottle costs $2.45.

To compare the prices, you need to know the price per ounce of each bottle. Divide the price by the weight in ounces:

$ .95 ÷ 16 fl. oz. = .059/ounce
$2.09 ÷ 38 fl. oz. = .055/ounce
$2.45 ÷ 48 fl. oz. = .051/ounce

Therefore, the largest size, 48 fl. oz., is the best buy because the price per ounce is the cheapest.

Comprehension Questions

Write the answers to the following questions.

1. What does unit price mean?

2. How can you determine the unit price of an item?

Listening Comprehension

A. Listen to the following conversations. Fill in the blanks based on the information in the conversation.

Example: Your teacher says:
Excuse me, can you tell me where the sugar is?
Yes, it's in Aisle 4, on the middle shelf, between the flour and nuts.

You write:
Item: _sugar_

Aisle: _4_

Shelf: _middle_

Between: _flour_   and   _nuts_

1. Item:_____

   Aisle:_____

   Shelf:_____

   Next to:_____

2. Item:_____

   Aisle:_____

   Shelf:_____

   Next to:_____

3. Item:_____

   Aisle:_____

   Shelf:_____

   Next to:_____

4. Item:_____

   Aisle:_____

   Shelf:_____

   Next to:_____

5. Item:_____

   Aisle:_____

   Shelf:_____

   Next to:_____

6. Item:_____

   Aisle:_____

   Shelf:_____

   Next to:_____

7. Item:_____

Aisle:_____

Shelf:_____

Next to:_____

8. Item:_____

Aisle:_____

Shelf:_____

Next to:_____

9. Item:_____

Aisle:_____

Shelf:_____

Next to:_____

10. Item:_____

Aisle:_____

Shelf:_____

Next to:_____

B. Listen to the following conversations. Fill in the blanks based on the information in the conversation.

Example: Your teacher says:
Excuse me, do you know how much this bag of sugar costs?
Yes, it's $1.29.

You write:
Item: _sugar_____

Price: _$1.29/bag_____

1. Item:_____

    Price:_____/_____

2. Item:_____

    Price:_____/_____

3. Item:_____

    Price:_____/_____

4. Item:_____

    Price:_____/_____

5. Item:_____

    Price:_____/_____

Problem Solving

Unit Pricing

Compare the prices of the following products. Determine the unit price. Which brand or size is the best buy?

Name of Product	Net Weight	Price	Unit Price	Best Buy
1. Clean-O Laundry Detergent				
Giant Size	49 oz. (3 lb. 1 oz.)	$2.05		
King Size	5 lb. 4 oz.	$3.35		
2. Wendell's Ketchup	14 oz.	$ .59		
	32 oz. (2 lb.)	$1.19		
	44 oz. (2 lb. 12 oz.)	$1.29		

Name of Product	Net Weight	Price	Unit Price	Best Buy
3. Willie Stargate Peanut Butter	12 oz.	$ .97		
	18 oz. (1 lb. 2 oz.)	$1.29		
	28 oz. (1 lb. 12 oz.)	$2.07		
	40 oz. (2 lb. 8 oz.)	$2.89		
4. Princess Cola	8 1-pt. (16 oz.) glass bottles	$2.29		
	32-fl.-oz. glass bottles	$ .69		
	67.6-fl.-oz. (2 qt. 3.6 oz.) plastic bottle	$1.39		
	6 12-fl.-oz. cans	$1.95		
5. Wishy-Washy Laundry Detergent				
King Size	6 lb. 4 oz.	$3.49		
Soapy Suds Laundry Detergent				
King Size	6 lb. 3 oz.	$3.25		
6. Uncle Brown's Mustard	24 oz. (1 lb. 8 oz.)	$ .79		
Grocery Shop Mustard	20½ oz. (1 lb. 4½ oz.)	$ .55		
7. Happy Hawaiian Pineapple Chunks	8 oz.	$ .41		
	15¼ oz.	$ .63		
Food Mart Pineapple Chunks	13¼ oz.	$ .51		
	20 oz. (1 lb. 4 oz.)	$ .73		

Unit Five

 # Supermarket Shopping

Learner Objectives

Consumer Competencies

Being able to recognize some advertising techniques used for supermarket products

Understanding the differences between "store brand" and "national brand"

Being able to read and compare the weekly newspaper advertisements for supermarkets and being able to determine the best place to shop

Being able to compare fresh, frozen, canned, and convenience foods for cost and nutritional value

Being able to recognize and use a coupon

Grammatical Structures

Being able to understand and use the comparative and superlative

Vocabulary Items

Being able to understand and use the following words in context:

Nouns	*Verbs*	delicious
advertiser	advertise	economical
advertising	lie	fresh
calories	persuade	frozen
convenience food	provide	in-season
coupon	taste	nutritious
expiration date		pre-cooked
fat	*Adjectives*	sliced
promotion	available	tasty
protein	balanced	
quality	canned	
value	convenient	
variety	cooked	
	cut up	

Dialogue

(in the Consumer Education class) Michael, the teacher, comes to class with two bags of groceries.

Michael:
Now that we know about supermarkets, let's learn how to choose the best and most economical products for you. Look at this jar of peanut butter. Who's on the label?

Ken:
Willie Stargate, the famous baseball player.

Michael:
Look at the ingredients.

Ken: *(reading the label)*
Peanuts, dextrose, vegetable oil, salt . . .

Michael:
Now, look at this store brand of peanut butter. Read the ingredients.

Cindy:
Peanuts, dextrose, vegetable oil, salt . . . Hey, they have the same ingredients.

Michael:
Right. Now, compare the prices. The two jars are the same size.

Ken:
$1.39 for the Willie Stargate brand.

Cindy:
The store brand is cheaper. It's only 99¢.

Michael:
Right, but more people buy the Willie Stargate brand than the store brand.

Cindy:
Why?

Lisa:
Because people want to eat the same peanut butter as Willie Stargate. They think that it's better for you and tastes better.

Michael:
Right. Advertisers pay Mr. Stargate for permission to put his picture on the label. Then they pass on the cost of the advertising and promotion to the consumer.

Lisa:
That's why store brands are usually cheaper. There's not as much advertising and promotion.

Michael:
Yes, but don't forget to compare labels and the unit prices. Now, compare these two boxes of cereal, Sugar Crunch and Wheat Flakes.

Barbara: *(comparing the labels)*
Sugar Crunch has more sugar than anything else. Wheat Flakes has more wheat. Wheat Flakes is more nutritious and has fewer calories.

Ron:
But, Michael, on TV it says that if you eat Sugar Crunch, you're eating a balanced breakfast.

Michael:
Think carefully about the ad on TV. What do they show?

Ron:
They show a bowl of Sugar Crunch with milk and fruit . . .

Barbara:
. . . a glass of juice, a glass of milk, and buttered toast.

Michael:
Then they say *this* breakfast—a bowl of Sugar Crunch with milk and fruit, a glass of juice, a glass of milk, and buttered toast—is a balanced breakfast.

Cindy:
Are they lying?

Michael:
No, advertisers can't lie. That's the law. But they want to convince you that their product is the best.

Lisa:
Yes, for example, in soft-drink ads, they always show pictures of young people having fun. You think if you drink that brand you're going to feel younger and have more fun.

Michael:
Now look at these two boxes of laundry detergent. One says Super Jumbo size, and the other box says Giant Economy size. Which box is bigger?

Ron:
The Super Jumbo size?

Michael:
Let's look at the net weights.

Ron:
They're both the same size!

Michael:
Right. Advertisers generally give you very little information about the product. They tell you their product is the tastiest, the most delicious, the biggest, the cheapest, or the most nutritious. But they usually don't give you any facts. They want you to believe that you *must* have their product. For example, if you want to feel younger, sexier, or nicer, you should use their product. Or if Willie Stargate eats the product, it must be good. When you shop, be careful. Be sure that you like the product. And be sure that it's the most economical for you.

Comprehension Questions

1. What's the class going to learn about?

2. Compare the Willie Stargate brand of peanut butter and the store brand. How are they similar? How are they different?

3. Why do more people buy the Willie Stargate brand?

4. Why is the Willie Stargate brand more expensive?

5. Is the store brand always cheaper and of the same quality as the national brand?

6. Compare Sugar Crunch and Wheat Flakes. How are they different?

7. Does Sugar Crunch alone provide a balanced breakfast?

8. Compare the Super Jumbo size and the Giant Economy size of laundry detergent. Are they different?

9. What kind of information do advertisers give you?

10. What do they want you to believe?

11. What should you be sure of when you shop?

12. What other methods do advertisers use to persuade you to buy their products?

Grammar Practice

Comparisons of Inequality

We can show that two people, things, or groups are different in some characteristic by using the comparative form of an adjective or adverb. To form the comparative we add *er* to one-syllable adjectives and adverbs and to two-syllable adjectives ending in *y*. Then we form a sentence using *than*.

Adjectives	(tall)	Mr. Jones is tall*er than* Mrs. Jones.
	(short)	Mrs. Jones is short*er than* Mr. Jones.
	(heavy)	Mr. Jones is heavi*er than* Mrs. Jones.*
Adverbs	(fast)	Shirley types fast*er than* Lisa.
	(slow)	Lisa types slow*er than* Shirley.

*In forming the comparative with two-syllable adjectives ending in *y*, the *y* must be changed to *i* before adding *er*.

Comparisons of Inequality: Exercises

A. Make sentences using the comparative form.

Example: Barbara is 24 years old. Cindy is 21 years old.

old: Barbara is *older than* Cindy.

young: Cindy is *younger than* Barbara.

1. Michael and Ken jog. Michael runs fast. Ken runs very fast.

   fast:

   slow:

2. Saturday the temperature was 60°. Sunday the temperature was 55°.

   warm:

   cool:

3. Ken and Lisa are having a fight. Ken is angry. Lisa is very angry.

   angry:

4. The store brand of peanut butter costs 99¢. The national brand costs $1.39.

   cheap:

5. Ken's 5′10″. Ron's 6′.

   tall:

   short:

6. Ron's happy today because he doesn't have to work. Cindy's very happy because she can spend the day with Ron.

   happy:

7. Ron was very busy at work yesterday. He had to fix a lot of cars. Yesterday was a slow day for Cindy at work.

   busy:

8. The King Size box of laundry detergent is 5 lb. 4 oz. The Giant Size box is 3 lb. 1 oz.

   large:

   small:

9. Mr. Jones weighs 200 lb. Mrs. Jones weighs 150 lb.

   heavy:

   light:

10. Barbara arrived at class at 8:00 p.m. Ken and Lisa arrived at 8:15 p.m.

    early:

    late:

11. Mr. Jones worked hard last week. Michael worked very hard.

    hard:

12. Food Mart's prices are low. Grocery Shop's prices are very low.

    low:

    high:

Some adjectives and adverbs have irregular comparative forms.

	Comparative
good	better than
well	better than
bad	worse than
badly	worse than

B. Fill in the blank with the comparative form.

1. People think the Willie Stargate brand of peanut butter is (good) _____

_____ the store brand.

2. Mr. Jones was sick yesterday. He feels (well) _____ today

_____ he did yesterday.

3. Mr. Jones felt (bad) _____ yesterday _____ he

did today.

To make comparisons with other adjectives, adverbs, and nouns, we can say the following:

Adjectives

Wheat Flakes is *more* nutritious *than* Sugar Crunch.
Sugar Crunch is *less* nutritious *than* Wheat Flakes.

Adverbs

Michael drives *more* carefully *than* Mr. Jones.
Mr. Jones drives *less* carefully *than* Michael.

Nouns

Sugar Crunch has *more* calories *than* Wheat Flakes.
Sugar Crunch has *more* sugar *than* Wheat Flakes.

Count:

Wheat Flakes has *fewer* calories *than* Sugar Crunch.

Noncount:

Wheat Flakes has *less* sugar *than* Sugar Crunch.

C. Make sentences using the comparative form. Follow the examples.

Example: Wheat Flakes contains a lot of wheat. Sugar Crunch contains some wheat.

wheat:

Wheat Flakes contains *more wheat than* Sugar Crunch.

Sugar Crunch contains *less wheat than* Wheat Flakes.

1. The store brand of orange drink contains 15% orange juice. The national brand contains 10% orange juice.

orange juice:

2. The store brand of peanut butter costs 99¢. The Willie Stargate brand costs $1.39.

   economical:

3. Ken drinks a cup of coffee for breakfast. Ron has a bowl of cereal, a glass of juice, and toast.

   balanced:

4. Barbara went to a party on Saturday. Michael worked.

   fun:

5. The Willie Stargate brand of peanut butter costs $1.39. The store brand costs 99¢.

   expensive:

6. The supermarket sells a lot of jars of the Willie Stargate brand of peanut butter. It sells some jars of its own.

   jars:

D. To determine the best place to shop, you should compare several things. Compare these two supermarkets. Which supermarket is better for you?

Food Mart	Grocery Shop
moderate prices	low prices
good variety of products and brands	fair variety of products and brands
all products usually available	some products not always available
five miles from your house	two miles from your house
can easily get there by bus	can't easily get there by bus
can pay by check	can't pay by check

Comparisons of Equality

When we want to show that two people or things are equal, we can say the following:

Nouns   The Willie Stargate brand of peanut butter is 18 oz. The store brand is also 18 oz.

The Willie Stargate brand is *the same* size *as* the store brand.

The two jars are *the same* size.

Ken drinks three cups of coffee a day. Lisa drinks three cups of coffee a day.

Count   Ken drinks *as many* cups of coffee a day *as* Lisa.

Noncount   Ken drinks *as much* coffee *as* Lisa.

Adjectives   Barbara is 23 years old. Ron is 23 years old.
               Barbara is *as old as* Ron.

Adverbs   Michael drives carefully. Ron drives carefully.
               Michael drives *as carefully as* Ron.

Comparisons of Equality: Exercises

Compare Barbara and her friend Jane. Use the information below.

Example: Barbara and Jane are the same age.
               Barbara is the same age as Jane.
               Barbara is as old as Jane.

Barbara
23 years old
5'5"
120 pounds
lives in a one-bedroom apartment
gets up at 6:30 a.m.
drinks two cups of coffee a day

Jane
23 years old
5'5"
120 pounds
lives in a one-bedroom apartment
gets up at 6:30 a.m.
drinks two cups of coffee a day

Superlative

To form the superlative we add -*est* to adjectives and adverbs that add -*er* in the comparative. *The* is placed before the adjective.

Adjectives	**Ron** 6′	**Michael** 5′11″	**Ken** 5′10″

Michael is tall*er* than Ken. (comparative)
Ron is *the* tall*est* of the three. (superlative)

Adverbs   Mr. Jones goes 70 mph on the highway. Ken goes 55 mph on the highway. Lisa goes 50 mph on the highway.

Ken drives fast*er* than Lisa.

Mr. Jones drives *the* fast*est*.

To form the superlative with other adjectives and adverbs and nouns we can say the following:

Adjectives   Wheat Flakes is *the most* nutritious cereal in the supermarket.

Sugar Crunch is *the least* nutritious cereal in the supermarket.

Adverbs   Ken drives *the most* carefully.

Mr. Jones drives *the least* carefully.

Nouns   Sugar Crunch has *the most* calories.

Sugar Crunch has *the most* sugar.

Count   Wheat Flakes has *the fewest* calories.

Noncount   Wheat Flakes has *the least* sugar.

Irregular Forms

	Comparative	**Superlative**
good	better than	the best
well	better than	the best
bad	worse than	the worst
badly	worse than	the worst

Superlative: Exercises

A. The items listed below are on special this week at these three supermarkets. Compare the unit prices. Which supermarket has the lowest prices this week?

Example:

	Super Market	Food Mart	Grocery Shop
Apples	39¢/lb.	$1.80/5-lb. bag	45¢/lb.

The apples at Super Market are cheaper than the apples at Grocery Shop. The apples at Food Mart are the cheapest.

	Super Market	Food Mart	Grocery Shop
Fresh Whole Chickens	57¢/lb.	68¢/lb.	59¢/lb.
Ground Beef	$1.55/lb.	$1.39/lb. (3 lb. or more)	$1.25/lb. (5 lb. or more)
Yellow Onions	$1/4 lb.	68¢/5-lb. bag	25¢/lb.
Lettuce	39¢/head	$1/3 heads	35¢/head
Chunk Tuna	69¢/6½-oz. can	69¢/6½-oz. can	65¢/6½-oz. can

B. Compare the following kinds of milk in terms of the four categories below.

Whole Milk	Lowfat Milk (2%)	Skim Milk
8 grams fat/8 oz.	5 grams fat/8 oz.	1 gram fat/8 oz.
150 calories/8 oz.	120 calories/8 oz.	100 calories/8 oz.
95¢/½ gal.	95¢/½ gal.	92¢/½ gal.

1. fat

2. calories

3. price

4. taste

C. Read the following paragraph.

Fresh, Frozen, or Canned?

How are fresh produce, frozen produce, and canned produce different? Generally, frozen fruits and vegetables are more nutritious than canned. Fresh fruits and vegetables are the most nutritious. Fresh produce can be the cheapest when it's in season. However, when it's not in season, it's usually the most expensive. Some products always cost less when they're frozen even when they're in season. For example, frozen orange juice is always cheaper than fresh orange juice. Frozen produce and canned produce are more convenient than fresh produce because they keep for a longer time in the freezer or kitchen cabinet. Sometimes they are easier to prepare because they're already cut up and cooked. However, some people think fresh produce tastes best. Other people like canned or frozen fruits and vegetables better. And others think fresh, frozen, and canned products taste the same.

Based on the reading above, compare fresh, frozen, and canned fruits and vegetables using the following words.

1. nutritious

2. cheap

3. expensive

4. economical

5. convenient

6. easy

7. delicious

D. Compare the following items for unit price, taste, and nutrition. (Don't forget that the net weight of canned fruits and vegetables includes the liquid in the can.)

Example: *Fresh spinach is more expensive than canned spinach and frozen spinach, but fresh spinach is the most nutritious.*

	Fresh	Frozen	Canned
Mushrooms	$1.89/16 oz.	$1.09/6 oz. (in butter sauce)	$1.05/8 oz. (stems & pieces)
Carrots	33¢/lb.	41¢/10 oz.	39¢/9 oz.
Green Beans	79¢/lb.	49¢/9 oz. (cut)	59¢/16 oz. (cut)
Spinach	89¢/lb.	35¢/10 oz.	59¢/16 oz.
Pears	89¢/lb.		69¢/16 oz. (sliced)

Reading

Coupons

We use coupons to save money on certain products. You can find coupons in the Food section of the newspaper usually on Wednesday or Thursday and Sunday. You should use coupons only for products that you normally buy. You can also use a coupon to try something new. Then you should buy the smallest size.

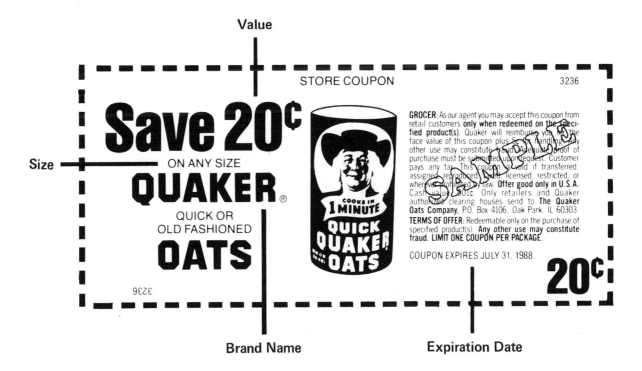

Value

Size

Brand Name

Expiration Date

Value

The value of the coupon is the money you save when you buy the product and use the coupon. The value is written: "Save 20¢," "15¢ off," or "This Coupon Worth 25¢." The value of this coupon is 20¢.

Brand Name

The coupon tells you the brand name of the product. This coupon is for Quaker Oats.

Size

The coupon tells you the size you must buy to use it. With this coupon you can buy any size of Quaker Oats.

Expiration Date

The expiration date is the last day you can use the coupon. The expiration date of this coupon is July 31, 1988.

Coupons are usually for national brands. Even with a coupon, the national brand can be more expensive than the store brand. For example, the national brand costs 89¢, and you have a coupon for 10¢. You pay only 79¢. However, the store brand costs only 69¢ and is of the same quality as the national brand. Therefore, even with a coupon, you pay a higher price for the national brand. Remember to compare unit prices.

Comprehension Questions

Write the answers to the following questions.

1. Where and when can you find coupons?

2. When should you use coupons?

3. What information is on a coupon?

4. Is the product that you buy with a coupon always the most economical? Why?

Convenience Foods

Convenience foods are sliced, cut up, or pre-cooked foods. Some convenience foods have the ingredients that you need in order to prepare the food in one box or package, for example, a cake mix or frozen broccoli in cheese sauce. Convenience foods take less time to prepare because the manufacturer did most of the preparation for you. However, convenience foods are usually less nutritious and cost more than preparing the food yourself.

If it is important for you to save time, you can use convenience foods. However, if you're interested in better quality, lower costs, and better nutrition, it's better to prepare the food yourself.

Comprehension Questions

Write the answers to the following questions.

1. What are convenience foods?

2. Why do convenience foods take less time to prepare?

3. What are the advantages of convenience foods?

4. What are the disadvantages of convenience foods?

Listening Comprehension

Listen to the following advertisements. Fill in the blanks based on the information in the advertisement.

Example: Your teacher says:
At Food Mart this week, large eggs, 59¢/dozen.

You write:

Supermarket: *Food Mart*

Item: *large eggs*

Price: *59¢/dozen*

1. Supermarket: _____

   Item: _____

   Price _____ / _____

2. Supermarket: _____

   Item: _____

   Price: _____ / _____

3. Supermarket: _____

   Item: _____

   Price: _____ / _____

4. Supermarket: _____

   Item: _____

   Price: _____ / _____

5. Supermarket: _____

   Item: _____

   Price: _____ / _____

6. Supermarket: _____

   Item: _____

   Price: _____ / _____

7. Supermarket: _____

   Item: _____

   Price: _____ / _____

8. Supermarket: _____

   Item: _____

   Price: _____ / _____

9. Supermarket: _____

   Item: _____

   Price: _____ / _____

10. Supermarket: _____

   Item: _____

   Price: _____ / _____

Unit Six

 # Looking for an Apartment

Learner Objectives

Consumer Competencies

Learning the steps in finding an apartment to rent

Learning how to read the classified housing ads in the newspaper

Learning what to consider when deciding on an apartment to rent

Grammatical Structures

Being able to understand and use the following structures: *would like, will, if. . .will,* and *may*

Vocabulary Items

Being able to understand and use the following words in context:

Nouns

air conditioning
appliance
appointment
bakery
block
bugs
carpeting
classified ad
cracks
damages
efficiency
electrical outlet
fee
fire escape
landlord

lease
lock
manager
neighborhood
plaster
real estate agency
repairs
security deposit
storage area
suburbs
tenant
want ad
water pressure
water stain

Verbs

afford
break
inspect
maintain
rent
repair

Adjectives

available
furnished/unfurnished
reasonable
wall-to-wall

Dialogue

Ron and Cindy are going to get married soon. They began to look at apartments last week.

(in the Consumer Education class)

Cindy:
Michael, Ron and I looked at apartments all last week.

Ron:
We looked everywhere—in the city, in the suburbs. . . . We can't decide. If we rent in the suburbs, we won't be able to take the bus. We'll have to drive. And you know the price of gas!

Cindy:
And we looked at every kind of apartment—one bedroom, two bedrooms. I can't remember what we've seen. And I'm confused. I don't understand security deposits, leases, and utilities. There must be a better way to look for an apartment!

Michael: *(laughing)*
Wait a minute! *Before* you begin looking, you should decide what kind of apartment you'd like and where you'd like to live. If you know what you want, it'll be easier to find a place, and you'll save time.

Cindy:
I'd like a two-bedroom apartment in the suburbs with a washer and dryer, air conditioning, a club house with a swimming pool, and tennis courts.

Ron:
Sure! And I'd like a villa on the French Riviera! Cindy, you know we can't afford that!

Michael:
Did you make a budget? Do you know how much you can afford?

Ron:
Well, no.

Michael:
First, decide how much you can afford. An apartment and the utilities should cost less than one third of your monthly take-home pay. Then you should decide what kind of apartment you want—one or two bedrooms, furnished or unfurnished. After you decide what kind of apartment you want, you can begin looking.

Ron:
That's a problem. How can we find out about apartments for rent?

Michael:
First, you should decide where you want to live—in the city or the suburbs, which neighborhood, near work, near the bus. Next, get a weekend newspaper and look at the classified ads.

Cindy:
You mean the want ads?

Michael:
Right.

Barbara:
There are other ways to find out about apartments. Drive or walk around the neighborhoods you like. Look for "for rent" signs. Stop in the neighborhood supermarkets and Laundromats. Sometimes they have bulletin boards with notices about apartments for rent.

Ken:
Talk to your friends or people at work. They may know about apartments for rent.

Lisa:
Some universities have housing offices. They have lists of apartments for rent.

Ken:
If you're in a hurry, check real estate agencies or apartment rental services. But some of them charge a fee, so you'll probably want to try the other ways first.

Michael:
Let's make a list of the ways to find an apartment: look at the want ads; drive or walk around the neighborhood; talk to friends and people at work; check the housing offices of universities; check real estate agencies or apartment rental services.

Comprehension Questions

1. According to Michael, what should you do before you begin looking at apartments? Why?

2. What kind of apartment would Cindy like? Is her wish reasonable?

3. How much should an apartment cost?

4. How can Cindy and Ron find out about apartments for rent?

5. What other ways can Ron and Cindy find out about apartments for rent?

Grammar Practice

Would Like

Would like is a polite way to say *want*. The contractions for *would like* are: I'd, you'd, he'd, she'd, it'd, we'd, you'd, they'd.

We ask:

> Would you like some coffee?
> Would you like to go to the movies?

We usually answer:

> Yes, please.   No, thank you.
> Sure.

The following short answers are not as common:

> Yes, I would.   No, I wouldn't.
> Yes, I'd like some.   No, I wouldn't like any.
> Yes, I'd like to.   No, I wouldn't like to.

Would Like: Exercises

A. Fill in the blanks of the questions with *Would you like*. Fill in the answers with *I'd like*.

1. In a real estate agency
    Manager: Can I help you?
    Customer: Yes,_____to rent an apartment.
    Agent: _____to rent a furnished or an unfurnished apartment?
    Customer: A furnished apartment.
    Agent: How many bedrooms_____ _____?
    Customer: One. But_____something in a safe neighborhood.
    Agent: Please fill out this card and sign here.

2. In a restaurant
    Waiter: _____anything from the bar?
    Customer: No, thank you.
    Waiter: Are you ready to order?
    Customer: No,_____a few more minutes.
    (Later)
    Waiter: _____to order now?
    Customer: Yes,_____the prime rib.
    Waiter: How_____it cooked?
    Customer: Medium rare.
    Waiter: Soup or salad?
    Customer: Salad.
    Waiter: What kind of salad dressing_____?
    Customer: What kind do you have?
    Waiter: French, thousand island, Roquefort...
    Customer: Roquefort.
    Waiter: Coffee?
    Customer: No,_____a glass of red wine.

3. On the telephone

Landlord:	Hello.
Customer:	Hello. _____ some information on the apartment for rent on Fifth Avenue.
Landlord:	It's a one-bedroom, unfurnished apartment for $350 a month including utilities.
Customer:	_____ to see it.
Landlord:	OK. Can you meet me there at one o'clock this afternoon?
Customer:	Yes, thank you.

B. Form questions with the following phrases and *Would you like (to)*. Answer the questions.

Example: see a menu
Would you like to see a menu?

Yes, please. or *No, thank you.* or *Yes, I would.* or *No, I wouldn't.*

1. sit down

2. something to drink

3. another cup of coffee

4. a one-bedroom or two-bedroom apartment

5. go to a museum or to the zoo tomorrow

C. Answer the question with *I'd like (to)* and the phrase.

Example: At a bakery.

May I help you?
Yes, (two dozen oatmeal cookies)

Yes, I'd like two dozen oatmeal cookies.

1. At a furniture store.
   Salesperson: May I help you?
                   Yes, (look at a sofa).

2. At the library.
   Librarian: May I help you?
                     Yes, (check out these books).

3. At an appliance store.
   Salesperson: May I help you?
                     Yes, (look at a washing machine).

4. At the ticket office.
   May I help you?
   Yes, (two tickets for the symphony on Friday night).

5. At an ice cream shop.
   May I help you?
   Yes, (a double dip of chocolate chip).

D. Role-play the following situations.

1. You want to open a savings account. Tell the bank manager what you want.

2. You want to look at a used car. Tell the salesperson.

3. You want to withdraw $50 from your bank account. Tell the teller.

4. You want to place a collect call to your parents. Tell the telephone operator.

5. You want to speak to the director of the company. Tell the secretary.

6. You want some information about an apartment for rent. Tell the apartment manager.

7. You're at a fast-food restaurant. You want a double hamburger, small fries, and a large Coke. Tell the waitress or waiter.

E. Newspapers use abbreviations in the want ads in order to save space. You need to understand the abbreviations in order to understand the ad. Look at the following abbreviations.

apt	apartment	DR	dining room
a/c	air conditioning	effcy	efficiency
avail imm	available immediately	elec	electricity
BR	bedroom	eves	evenings
blk	block	exc	excellent
bldg	building	fl	floor
carp	carpeting	furn/unfurn	furnished/unfurnished

gar	garage	prkg	parking
ht	heat	priv	private
incl or inc	includes	refs	references
kit	kitchen	refrig	refrigerator
laund	laundry	rm	room
lge	large	sec bldg	security building
LR	living room	utils	utilities
loc	location	w/w *or* ww	wall-to-wall carpeting
nr	near	w/	with

Now use the abbreviations above to tell what kind of apartment these people would like.

Example:

Steve: 1 BR unfurn suburbs $300/month

Steve would like a one-bedroom, unfurnished apartment in the suburbs for $300 a month.

1. Robert: effcy furn nr university $180/month incl utilities

2. The Hamiltons: 2 BR DR w/w a/c sec bldg w/gar $525/month

3. Gloria: 1 BR unfurn laund nr bus avail imm $225/month

4. Dan: 2 BR unfurn DR nr school $425/month

F. Read these ads.

1. Suburban: Lge 1 BR, w/w, laund $280 + elec. 217-3241 eves.

2. South Hills: 2 BR, DR, w/w, nr park and bus $325 + utils. 415-6829

3. East End: Lge furn 1 rm effcy in priv home. Refs. nr bus $180. 924-5631

4. City: 1 BR, 1½ baths w/river view $900 inc ht. Avail imm. 323-4129

Now match the descriptions below with the right ad.

Example:

Tom works in the city but would like to live in the suburbs. He'd like a one-bedroom apartment for about $300.

Ad #1.

a. Ms. Forbes is very rich. She'd like an apartment with a good view.

b. Jane works in the South Hills. She'd like to share an apartment with a friend. Her take-home pay is $750 a month.

c. Gary is a student. He doesn't have a lot of money. He'd like to pay about $160 a month for a furnished apartment.

d. Mr. Miller doesn't have a car. He'd like to live with a family.

G. Look at the following ads. Form sentences with _____ *'d like* to match the ads.

Example:

South Side: Modern apt. 1 blk bus 1st fl $195

I'd like an apartment for under $200 near the bus.

1. West End: Effcy, 1 & 2 BR's avail for May or June, w/w, a/c, sec bldg. Exc loc. 424-9175

2. Suburban: 1 BR, laund, w/w carp, utils incl $285 prkg. avail. No children/pets 395-5687

3. North Side: 2nd fl, 1 BR, LR, bath, lge kit, lge refrig. Nr bus May 1st $435 + ht 217-9354

4. City: 2 BR a/c, w/w, laund, gar avail $350 incl ht 419-2742

Will

Will indicates an action in the future. The affirmative contractions are: I'll, you'll, he'll, she'll, it'll, we'll, you'll, they'll. The negative contraction is *won't*.

Question
Will Ron and Cindy rent an apartment soon?

Answers
Yes, they'll rent an apartment soon.

No, they won't rent an apartment soon.

Short Answers
Yes, they will.

No, they won't.

Some time-expressions that we use with *will* are:

next week, next month, next year, next Sunday

in a few minutes, in a week, later

tomorrow, the day after tomorrow

Will: **Exercises**

A. In ads, companies make promises about what their products will do for you. Fill in the blanks with *You'll.*

1. Eat Willie Stargate Peanut Butter! _____ feel like a star!

2. Take Ache-less Aspirin! _____ feel better fast!

3. Buy Super Jumbo Clean-O Laundry Detergent! _____ have a cleaner

   wash, and _____ save money!

4. Munch on Munchy Potato Chips! _____ love the taste!

5. Buy Purrr-fume! _____ feel sexier!

Tell what these products will do for you.

6. Use Silky Hands Dishwashing Liquid!

7. Drive a Speed-O Sports Car!

8. Brush your teeth with Horizon Toothpaste!

B. Before you rent an apartment, you should ask the landlord some questions. Fill in the blanks of these questions with *will*.

1. Who _____ make the repairs?

2. Who _____ paint the apartment?

3. Who _____ fix the appliances (stove, refrigerator, oven) if they break?

4. _____ the landlord raise the rent?

5. How much _____ the utilities cost a month?

C. Fill in the blank of the question with *will*. Fill in the blank of the answer with a pronoun and *will*. Use contractions.

Example:
When *will* Ron and Cindy make a budget?

They'll make a budget before they look for an apartment.

1. How _____ Ron and Cindy find out about apartments for rent?

_____ look in the newspaper.

2. When _____ we see you again? _____ see you next week.

3. Where _____ Fred open a bank account? _____ open a bank account at First National Bank.

4. How much money _____ Ron and Cindy deposit in their savings account?

_____ deposit $50.

5. What _____ Ken buy at the supermarket? _____ buy 20 lb. of laundry detergent.

6. When _____ the store open? _____ open at 10 a.m.

D. Form questions with *will* and the following phrases. Answer the questions.

Example: look for an apartment.

Will Ron and Cindy look for an apartment tomorrow?
No, they won't. They'll look for an apartment this weekend.

1. rent an apartment

2. go to the supermarket

3. open a bank account

4. cash a check

5. pay your bills

E. Tell what will happen in the future.

Example:

Ken's not going to buy steak at the supermarket this week.

He'll buy hamburger.

1. Ron and Cindy aren't going to look for an apartment today.

2. Ken and Lisa aren't going to clean the house today.

3. Ron isn't going to finish fixing the car today.

4. Ron and Cindy aren't going to buy a house.

5. Mrs. Jones isn't going to start her diet today.

6. I'm not going to study English this morning.

7. We're not going to the movies tonight.

If...Will

We use the expression *if...will* to show that one action depends on another action. The verb after *if* is usually in the present tense. We use *will* in the main part of the sentence.

> If it rains tomorrow, will you go swimming?
> If it rains tomorrow, we won't go swimming.
> If it's sunny tomorrow, we'll go swimming.

We can put the *if*-clause at the beginning or at the end of the sentence:

> If I have time tomorrow, I'll look for an apartment.
> I'll look for an apartment if I have time tomorrow.

If...will: **Exercises**

A. Fill in the blanks with *will* or *won't*.

If you decide to rent an apartment, you should first determine what kind of apartment you

would like. If you know what you want, it _____ be easier to find a place,

and you _____ save time. Careful planning _____ help

you. However, you probably _____ find the exact apartment that you

want. If you rent an apartment, your main cost _____ be your monthly

rent. You _____ also have to pay some utilities. The rent and the utilities

shouldn't cost more than one third of your monthly take-home pay. You probably

_____ have to pay a security deposit. The security deposit is usually equal

to one or two months' rent. The landlord _____ use the security deposit to pay

for repairs of the damages that you cause and to clean the apartment after you leave. He

_____ also keep it if you move away from the apartment without paying. If

you leave the apartment in good condition, the landlord _____ return your

security deposit. If you don't clean your apartment, you _____ probably

lose the security deposit.

If you look in the newspaper, you _____ find a list of apartments for rent

in the classified ads. When you see an apartment that looks interesting, you should call

the landlord or manager (the manager takes care of the apartment building). You should

make an appointment to see the apartment.

B. Answer the questions based on the information in the reading.

    1. Will you always find the exact apartment that you want?

    2. What will your main cost be if you rent an apartment?

    3. What else will you have to pay?

    4. What will the landlord use the security deposit for?

    5. Will the landlord return your security deposit?

    6. What will you find if you look in the classified ads of the newspaper?

C. Complete these sentences and questions. Use contractions when possible.

    Example:

        If Ron and Cindy _rent_ (rent) an apartment in the suburbs, they_'ll have_ (have) to drive to work.

    1. If I _____ (have) time, I _____ (call) you tonight.

    2. Lisa _____ (wash) the dishes if Ken _____ (do) the laundry.

    3. If you _____ (go) to the store, _____ you _____ (buy) some milk?

    4. If I _____ (rent) this apartment, how much _____ the rent _____ (be)?

    5. If it _____ (be) sunny tomorrow, Barbara _____ (go) to the beach.

D. Answer the questions.

    1. If you go home from class by bus, how long will it take?

    2. What will you do if you miss the bus?

    3. If you aren't tired, what will you do after class?

    4. If you go to the supermarket today, what will you buy?

    5. How much will the security deposit be if you rent an apartment?

    6. If you don't pay your rent, what will your landlord do?

E. Form questions with these phrases. Answer them.

    Example: If it rains this weekend,

                  If it rains this weekend, will you go to the movies?

                  No, I won't. I'll go to a museum.

    1. If Ron and Cindy open a savings account,

    2. If you like the apartment on 5th Avenue,

    3. If Ron and Cindy rent an apartment near their jobs,

    4. If Barbara buys a new car,

    5. If Ron and Cindy rent an unfurnished apartment,

May

May has three meanings.

1. We use *may* to make a request. It is very polite.

> Salesperson: May I help you?
>
> Customer: Yes, I'd like to look at a color TV.

2. We use *may* to ask permission. It is very polite.

> Student: May I leave the class early?
>
> Teacher: Yes, you may.
>
> No, you may not.

3. We use *may* to show possibility.

> I'm not sure if I'll go to the beach tomorrow. It may rain.

We use *may* + the simple form of the verb. We use *may* for the present (You *may* go now) and we use *may* for the future (It *may* snow tomorrow).

May: Exercises

A. Fill in the blank with *may*.

1. It _____ rain tomorrow, but I don't really think it will.

2. Johnny's mother said he _____ have another cookie.

3. Barbara's absent from class this evening. She _____ be sick.

4. Ron and Cindy can't decide where to rent an apartment. They _____ rent

   in the city, or they _____ rent in the suburbs.

5. When you rent an apartment, you _____ have to pay all the utilities, or

   you _____ only have to pay for the telephone.

6. The sign says "No Smoking." You _____ not smoke.

7. My mother wrote me a letter three days ago. I _____ receive it today.

8. I'm not sure where Michael is. He _____ be in the library.

B. Tell what Ron and Cindy may do this weekend.

Example: go to the movies

Ron and Cindy may go to the movies this weekend.

1. look for an apartment

2. go shopping

3. rent an apartment

4. look at furniture

5. go to the mountains

C. Make questions with *may* for the following situations.

Example: You want to leave class early because you don't feel well. Ask the teacher.

May I leave class early tonight?

1. You work in a clothing store. A customer comes in. What do you say?

2. You're knocking on your friend's door. You want to enter the room. What do you say?

3. You want to borrow your boss's pen. What do you say?

4. You're cold. You want to close the window in the classroom. Ask the teacher.

5. You're calling on the telephone. You want to speak to Mrs. Forbes. What do you say?

Listening Comprehension

Listen to the following conversations. Answer the questions based on the information in the conversations.

A. A conversation between Ron and the apartment manager.

   1. Is Ron interested in a one- or two-bedroom apartment?

   2. Where's it located?

   3. Is it furnished?

   4. How much is the rent?

   5. Does the rent include all utilities?

   6. Does Ron want to see the apartment?

B. A conversation between Dan and the apartment manager.

   1. How many bedrooms does the apartment have?

   2. Does the apartment have carpeting?

   3. Do they permit children?

   4. Where's the apartment located?

   5. How much is the rent?

   6. Does Dan want to see the apartment?

C. A conversation between Robert and the apartment manager.

1. What kind of apartment is it?

2. Is it furnished?

3. Is it near the university?

4. How much is the rent?

5. Does Robert want to see it? Why?

Reading

Looking for an Apartment

Before you look at an apartment, you should find out the answers to the following questions by calling the landlord or manager.

1. How much is the rent?

2. Does the rent include the cost of the utilities? If not, how much do the utilities cost during the summer and the winter?

3. Is there a security deposit? How much is it? In most cities, the security deposit cannot legally be more than two months' rent.

4. Are there any other fees, for example, a parking fee or a cleaning fee? Do you have to pay the last month's rent in advance?

5. Where's the apartment located? Is it near your job, shopping, and the bus?

6. Is there a lease (a written agreement between you and the landlord)? How long is it for? Can it be broken?

7. Do they allow children and pets?

When you look at an apartment, you should consider the following factors.

Neighborhood
Is the neighborhood safe, clean, quiet, and well-lighted?

Is the apartment close to stores, your job, schools, a Laundromat, and the bus?

Building
Is the building clean?

Are there locks on outside doors?

Are there fire escapes?

Are there parking places or a garage? Are they well-lighted?

Are there storage areas, laundry facilities? Are they clean?

Is there a mailbox for each tenant?

Apartment
Do you like the floor plan?

Are the rooms large enough for your furniture?

Are there locks on all outside doors?

Do the windows have locks? Are the windows broken? Do they let in enough air and light?

Do doors and windows open and close easily?

Do the lighting fixtures work? Is there enough light?

Are there enough electrical outlets?

Is the apartment quiet? Can you hear the neighbor's TV or children? Can you hear traffic?

Are the walls, ceilings, and floors in good condition? Do they have cracks, loose plaster, or water stains?

Are there drapes and carpets? Are they clean?

Does the heat work? Is there an air conditioner? Does it work?

Are there enough closets, cabinets, and storage areas?

Is the apartment free of bugs?

Do the kitchen appliances work? Who is responsible for repairing them?
Are they clean? Is the refrigerator big enough?

Does everything in the bathroom work? Is there enough water pressure? Is there enough hot water?

After you have inspected the apartment, you should try to talk to some of the other tenants. Ask them if there is enough heat and hot water and if the apartment building is free of bugs. Ask them if the landlord maintains the building well and if he makes repairs quickly.

Comprehension Questions

1. What should you find out before you look at an apartment?

2. When are your utility bills the highest?

3. How much can the security deposit legally be?

4. What's a lease?

5. What will your initial costs be when you rent an apartment?

6. What should you check in the neighborhood?

7. What should you check in the building?

8. What should you check in the apartment?

9. Why should you try to talk to some of the other tenants?

Unit Seven

Renting an Apartment

Learner Objectives

Consumer Competencies

Learning the steps in renting an apartment, for example, signing a lease, moving, landlord and tenant responsibilities

Learning what to do in case of a housing problem

Grammatical Structures

Being able to understand and use the present perfect tense

Vocabulary Items

Being able to understand and use the following words in context:

Nouns	Verbs
change-of-address card	forward
credit rating	initial
deposit	notify
homeowner's insurance	promise
initials	run into
installation fee	sublet
liability insurance	
refund	
theft	

Dialogue

Secretary: *(on the telephone)*
Acme Realty Company.

Barbara:
May I speak to Mr. Sellers, please?

Secretary:
He's not in right now. May I take a message?

Barbara:
Yes. This is Barbara Graham. I live at 1727 Walnut Street. I've called Mr. Sellers several times already about the heat in my apartment. I can't turn it off. Mr. Sellers promised to send someone to fix it, but no one has come yet.

Secretary:
I'll give him the message.

Barbara:
Thank you. Bye.

(Barbara runs into Michael later in the supermarket. They greet each other.)

Barbara:
Michael, do you have a minute? I have a problem with my landlord.

Michael:
Sure, Barbara. What's the problem?

Barbara:
It's about 85° outside, and my landlord hasn't turned off the heat yet. I've called him several times, but he hasn't fixed it yet. I know he has to provide adequate heat, but this is ridiculous! It's hotter in my apartment than it is outside.

Michael:
What did he say when you called him?

Barbara:
I talked to him a few weeks ago, and he promised to send someone to repair it within a week. I've called him again several times, but he's never in.

Michael:
Have you written him a letter?

Barbara:
No, I haven't. Should I?

Michael:
Yes. You should write him a letter after you talk to him on the phone. In the letter, repeat what he promised you on the phone. For example: Dear Mr. _____. What's his name?

Barbara:
Sellers.

Michael:
Dear Mr. Sellers,
When we talked yesterday *(give the date),* you promised to send someone to fix the heat within a week. Please tell me when the repairer is coming.
Sincerely,
Barbara Graham

Be sure to keep a copy of the letter.

Barbara:
I'll have to write him a letter immediately. What should I do if he still won't fix it?

Michael:
Then you can call a lawyer. Laws vary from city to city, so you need to find out the local law. You can also call the Legal Aid Society, a tenants' organization, or the Urban League. They can help you decide what you should do next.

Barbara:
Thanks a lot, Michael. You've been a big help.

Michael:
Sure, Barbara, good luck.

Comprehension Questions

1. Who's Barbara calling?

2. Is he there?

3. Why is she calling?

4. Who does Barbara see in the supermarket?

5. Why does Barbara want her landlord to turn off the heat?

6. What did her landlord promise her?

7. What should Barbara write in the letter?

8. What should Barbara do if the landlord still won't fix the heat?

Grammar Practice

Present Perfect

We use the present perfect to show:

1. an action that began in the past and continues to the present:
> Ken has lived in Pittsburgh for five years.

2. an action that occurred at an indefinite time in the past:
> I have visited New York before.

We form the present perfect with the auxiliary *have* and the past participle. The past participle is the same verb form as the past tense for regular verbs.

Affirmative

I have looked

you have looked

he, she, it has looked

we have looked

you have looked

they have looked

Contractions: I've, you've, he's, she's, it's, we've, you've, they've

Negative

I have not looked

you have not looked

he, she, it has not looked

we have not looked

you have not looked

they have not looked

Contractions: I haven't, you haven't, he hasn't, she hasn't, it hasn't, we haven't, you haven't, they haven't

Question Form

Have I looked?

Have you looked?

Has he looked?

Has she looked?

Has it looked?

Have we looked?

Have you looked?

Have they looked?

Short Answers

Affirmative

Yes, I have.

Yes, you have.

Yes, he has.

Yes, she has.

Yes, it has.

Yes, we have.

Yes, they have.

Negative

No, I haven't.

No, you haven't.

No, he hasn't.

No, she hasn't.

No, it hasn't.

No, we haven't.

No, they haven't.

Some irregular verbs have the same forms for the past and the past participles (see *find*). Other irregular verbs have a past participle form that is different from its present and past (see *write*). Those that are used in this unit are as follows:

Present	Past	Past Participle
be	was, were	been
buy	bought	bought
come	came	come
do	did	done
find	found	found
make	made	made
read	read	read
see	saw	seen
teach	taught	taught
write	wrote	written

Present Perfect: Exercises

A. Fill in the blanks with the correct form of the verb in the present perfect.

Example:　　Ron and Cindy *have looked* (look) at apartments all week.

1. Ken and Lisa _____ (live) in Pittsburgh for five years.

2. The class _____ already _____ (learn) about shopping in supermarkets.

3. Barbara _____ (attend) the Consumer Education class since October.

4. Ron and Cindy _____ recently _____ (look) in the want ads for apartments for rent.

B. Fill in the blanks with the negative form of the verb in the present perfect.

Example:　　I *haven't listened* (listen) to the radio for three days.

1. Mr. and Mrs. Jones _____ (watch) TV all evening.

2. Ron and Cindy _____ (call) about the apartment on Grant Street yet.

3. You _____ (smoke) a cigarette for five months.

C. Form questions in the present perfect tense. Answer them.

Example: How long *have you lived* (live) in your house?

1. How long _____ (study) English?

2. How long _____ (work) at your present job?

3. How many apartments _____ (look) at this week?

4. How long _____ (live) in the United States?

5. How many times _____ (be) to a baseball game?

6. How many questions _____ (answer) so far?

D. Answer the questions with a short answer.

Example: Have you lived in Pittsburgh all your life?

   Yes, I have.

1. Have you lived in the United States for a long time?

2. Have you studied English for a long time?

3. Has your English improved since you've been in the United States?

4. Have you ever visited Canada?

5. Have Ron and Cindy looked for an apartment lately?

6. Have you done your laundry recently?

7. Have you seen a good movie lately?

E. Form questions with *How long.* Answer them with *since* and with *for.*

Example: Fred, the ex-bank robber, is in jail. The judge sent him to jail six months ago.

How long has Fred been in jail?
He's been in jail for six months.
He's been in jail since January.

1. Ken and Lisa live in Pittsburgh. They moved to Pittsburgh five years ago.

2. Lisa's a university professor. In 1978 she began working at the university.

3. Michael teaches the Consumer Education class. He began teaching the class in October.

4. Ron's a car mechanic. He began working as a car mechanic three years ago.

5. José studies English. He began studying English three years ago.

F. Ask your classmates questions with *How long* and these phrases.

Example: live in Pittsburgh

How long have you lived in Pittsburgh?

1. study English

2. be in the U.S.

3. live at your present address

4. be married

G. Barbara has decided to look for a new apartment because she doesn't like her landlord, and she wants a larger apartment. Ask questions to find out if she's done the following things to look for an apartment. Answer the questions.

Example: look in the newspaper

Has Barbara looked in the newspaper yet?

Yes, she's already looked in the newspaper.

(No, she hasn't looked in the newspaper yet).

1. read the want ads

Yes,

2. walk around the neighborhood

Yes,

3. talk to friends and people at work

Yes,

4. call a real estate agency

No,

5. check the housing office at the university

No,

6. find an apartment

No,

7. sign a lease

No,

H. Ron and Cindy have finally found an apartment. Ron is getting ready to move out of his old apartment and into the new one. Ask questions to find out what he has already done and what he hasn't done yet. Answer the questions.

Example: open a bank account near his new apartment

Has Ron opened a bank account near his new apartment yet?

No, *he hasn't.*

1. notify magazine publishers of his new address

Yes,

2. write to friends to tell them his new address

Yes,

3. change the address on his driver's license

No,

4. call the telephone company

Yes,

NOTE:	Ron doesn't have to pay the telephone company a deposit because he has always paid his telephone bills on time. He has a good credit rating with the telephone company. He will have to pay the telephone company a fee to begin telephone service in his new apartment. This is called an installation fee.
	If you've never had a telephone in your own name, the company will probably ask you to pay a deposit for new service.

5. call the electric company

Yes,

6. make notes on the condition of the apartment

Yes,

> **NOTE:**   Before you move into an apartment, make notes on the condition of the apartment, the appliances, and any furniture included in the apartment. If possible, ask the landlord to look at the apartment with you. Sign and date the notes. Ask the landlord to sign them also. Keep a copy and give one to the landlord.

7. buy homeowner's insurance for the new apartment

No,

> **NOTE:**   It is a good idea to get homeowner's insurance to protect your personal property against fire and theft. Homeowner's insurance can also include liability insurance. Liability insurance protects you if someone has an accident in your home. You can buy homeowner's insurance if you own or rent an apartment or house.

8. pay the rent and security deposit for the new apartment

Yes,

9. receive the security deposit from the landlord of his old apartment

No,

10. fill out a change-of-address card

Yes,

> **NOTE:**   The change-of-address card is a form you fill out at the post office. The post office will forward your mail. This means they will send your mail to your new address if it has your old address on it.

I. Here is a copy of the change-of-address card that Ron filled out. Answer the questions.

THIS ORDER PROVIDES for the forwarding of First-Class Mail and all parcels of obvious value for a period not to exceed 1 year.	Print or Type *(Last Name, First Name, Middle Initial)* **Evans, Ronald W.**
CHANGE OF ADDRESS IS FOR: ☐ Entire Family *(When last name of family members differ, separate orders for each last name must be filed)* ☒ Individual Signer Only	OLD ADDRESS — No. and St., Apt., Suite, P.O. Box or R.D. No. (In care of) **412 40th St.**
I AGREE TO PAY FORWARDING POSTAGE FOR NEWSPAPERS AND MAGAZINES FOR 90 DAYS ☐ NO ☒ YES	Post Office, State and ZIP Code **Pittsburgh, PA 15222**
	NEW ADDRESS — No. and St., Apt., Suite, P.O. Box or R.D. No. (In care of) **592 Grant St. #4**
USPS USE ONLY CLERK/ CARRIER ENDORSEMENT	Post Office, State and ZIP Code **Pittsburgh, PA 15219**
CARRIER ROUTE NUMBER	Effective Date **6/25/91**	If Temporary, Expiration Date
DATE ENTERED	Sign Here ▶ *Ronald W. Evans*	Date Signed **6/19/91**

Signature & title of person authorizing address change. *(DO NOT print or type)*

1. Who filled out the card?

2. What's Ron's old address?

3. What's his new address?

4. When does Ron want the post office to begin forwarding his mail?

5. When did Ron fill out the card?

6. Is the change-of-address for Ron and his family or only for him?

7. Does Ron want to pay the post office to forward his magazines and newspapers?

J. Ask your classmates if, at any time in their lives, they have done the following things.

   Example: go to the zoo

   Have you ever gone to the zoo?

   No, never. or *Yes, I have.* or *No, I haven't.*

   1. fill out a change-of-address card

   2. call the telephone company

   3. buy homeowner's insurance

   4. sign a lease

   5. write a letter of complaint to your landlord

   6. be late for class

   7. sail a boat

   8. see a tornado

Listening Comprehension

Listen to the following conversations. Answer the questions based on the information in the conversation.

A. Mr. Sellers, Barbara's landlord, calls her on the phone.

   1. Who's calling Barbara?

   2. Why is he calling?

3. When will the repairman be at Barbara's apartment?

4. Will Barbara be there?

B. Ron's talking on the phone with the landlord.

   1. Why is Ron calling Mr. Lesser?

   2. When should Ron be at Mr. Lesser's office?

   3. Why is Ron going to Mr. Lesser's office?

C. Ron calls an insurance company to find out some information about homeowner's insurance for the new apartment.

   1. What's the first question the insurance agent asks Ron?

   2. How many apartment units are there in Ron and Cindy's building?

   3. What floor do Ron and Cindy live on?

   4. Is the building brick or frame?

   5. How much will personal property insurance cost?

   6. How much will liability insurance cost?

Reading

Leases

A lease is a written agreement between the landlord and tenant. Be sure you read the lease carefully *before* you sign it. Never sign a lease that you can't read. If you need help in reading the lease, you can call one of the following. They'll help you.

1. a lawyer
2. the Urban League
3. the Legal Aid Society or Neighborhood Legal Services
4. tenants' organizations

A lease should contain the following information:

1. Your name and the address of the apartment.
2. The name, address, and telephone number of the landlord and the manager.
3. How much rent you must pay and to whom you must pay it.
4. When the rent is due.
5. How long the lease is for; when it begins and when it ends.
6. How much the security deposit is; if there are any other fees.
7. What utilities you must pay; what utilities the landlord must pay.

The landlord and tenant have responsibilities. The lease will usually list these responsibilities.

Tenant Responsibilities

1. You must pay your rent on time.
2. You must take care of the apartment. Don't put holes in the walls, paint the floor, etc.
3. You must not cause fire or health problems.

Before you sign the lease, you should find out:

- if you can sublet the apartment;
- what will happen if you break the lease;
- if you can have children or pets in the apartment;
- what repairs you will be responsible for;
- if you have any other responsibilities.

Landlord Responsibilities

1. The landlord must take care of the building and grounds. For example, he must cut the grass, repair the roof, etc.

2. The landlord must provide heat, hot water, and keep the building free of bugs. That is the law.

3. The lease will tell you when the landlord can enter your apartment.

Before you sign the lease, find out what repairs the landlord will be responsible for.

If you or the landlord wants to change the lease, write the changes on the lease. You and the landlord should initial the changes (your initials are the first letters of your full name). Also, if the landlord makes any promises, for example, if he promises to paint the apartment before you move in, write it on the lease and initial it. Never sign a lease that has any blank spaces.

After you understand the lease completely, you and the landlord should sign two copies. You keep a copy, and the landlord keeps a copy.

At the end of the lease, the landlord can: (1) raise the rent; (2) ask you to move; (3) renew your lease. Of course, you may decide to move. If you decide to move, you should go through the apartment with the landlord to determine the damages that you are responsible for. In many states, the law requires the landlord to give you within 30 days after you move out:

1. a list of any repairs that you are responsible for.

2. a refund of your security deposit less the cost of repairs on the list.

Comprehension Questions

Write the answers to the following questions.

1. What's a lease?

2. Should you sign a lease that you don't understand?

3. What should you do if you don't understand a lease?

4. What information should a lease contain?

5. What responsibilities does a tenant have?

6. What should you find out before you sign a lease?

7. What responsibilities does the landlord have?

8. What should you do if you or the landlord changes the lease or if the landlord makes any promises?

9. When should you sign the lease?

10. What's the law in your city or state concerning security deposits?

Unit Eight

 # Buying Furniture and Appliances

Learner Objectives

Consumer Competencies

Learning the steps involved in buying furniture and appliances

Learning about the different types of stores where you can buy furniture and appliances

Being able to recognize different sales tactics

Grammatical Structures

Review of the following verb tenses: present; present continuous; past; past continuous; future (*going to* + verb; *will* + verb); and present perfect

Vocabulary Items

Being able to understand and use the following words in context:

Nouns

annual percentage rate	fee	service
charge account	finance charge	specialty store
complaint	finance company	warranty
consumer guides	fine print	
credit	garage sale	*Verbs*
credit contract	installation	fire
credit plan	installment plan	measure
delivery	interest rates	
department store	manufacturer	*Adjective*
discount store	model	reputable
down payment	operation	
durability	secondhand store	

Dialogue

(in the Consumer Education class)

Ron:
Michael, Cindy and I have decided to buy a sofa for our new apartment. Can you tell us how to go about looking for one?

Michael:
Weren't you going to rent a furnished apartment?

Ron:
We were, but we compared the cost of renting a furnished apartment with the cost of buying furniture. We've saved some money. We're going to get wedding gifts, and our parents are going to give us some things. So, we decided to rent an unfurnished apartment. It'll be cheaper in the long run. And if we buy a house someday, we'll already have furniture.

Ken:
Michael, Lisa and I want to buy a washing machine and dryer. With the baby coming, we'll need them.

Barbara:
And I want to buy a TV. How do we go about it?

Michael:
Basically, you follow the same steps to buy a sofa, a washing machine, or a TV. First, you must decide if you really need what you're thinking about buying.

Cindy, Ken, Barbara:
Yes!

Michael:
OK. Then let's discuss how to go about buying furniture and appliances and where to buy them. There are four basic steps: decide how much you can or want to spend; plan before you shop; learn everything you can about the product; compare prices and services at different stores.

Cindy:
This will be a big help.

Ron:
Yes. Then after we find out how to shop and where to shop, all we have to do is figure out how to pay for it!

Comprehension Questions

1. Why did Cindy and Ron decide to rent an unfurnished apartment?

2. What do Ken and Lisa want to buy? Why?

3. What does Barbara want to buy?

4. What do you have to decide first before you buy furniture and appliances?

5. What are the basic steps for buying furniture and appliances?

6. What does Ron want to know after he finds out how and where to shop?

Grammar Practice

Tense Review

A. Fill in the blanks with the correct form of the verb.

Barbara *is going* to a department store today to look for a TV. She _____

(have) a charge account at the department store, so she _____ (know) if she

_____ (find) a TV, she can _____ (use) her credit card. The

department store _____ (have) a good variety of TV's and it

_____ (offer) many services.

    Yesterday, Barbara _____ (go) to a specialty store. A specialty store

_____ (carry) one or a few different items. Some specialty stores

_____ (have) lower prices, and others _____ (have) higher

prices. They usually _____ (offer) good services. Barbara can

_____ (use) her credit card at a specialty store or the store's credit plan.

They _____ (have) the same interest rates.

    Barbara can also _____ (look) for a TV at a discount store. A discount

store usually _____ (sell) products at lower prices. Sometimes a discount

store _____ (not offer) as many services as a department store. And

sometimes the products in a discount store _____ (not be) as good as those in a department store. Barbara _____ (know) that she must

_____ (shop) carefully at a discount store.

Tomorrow Barbara _____ (call) a discount store to compare prices and

services. After Barbara compares prices and services at all the different stores, she

_____ (wait) a few weeks to see if the TV _____ (go) on

sale. Sometimes TV's _____ (be) cheaper on sale at a department store

than anywhere else.

Answer the questions based on the story.

1. Where is Barbara going today? Why?

2. What is the advantage of buying a TV at the department store?

3. Where did Barbara go yesterday?

4. How can Barbara pay for a TV at a specialty store?

5. What are the differences between a discount store and a department store?

6. Why should Barbara shop carefully at a discount store?

7. What will Barbara do after she compares prices and services at all the different stores?

8. When are TV's likely to be reasonably priced at a department store?

B. Ron and Cindy are thinking about using credit to buy their new sofa. However, they know they must use credit carefully. Read the story of how Fred became a bank robber. Fill in the blanks with the correct form of the verb.

Fred, the ex-bank robber, is out of jail now. He wants to buy a TV, but he doesn't have enough money. He can't use credit. That's how he got into trouble in the first place.

You see, Fred was married and _____ (have) a good job. Fred and his wife _____ (like) nice things. So they _____ (buy) a lot.

When they _____ (not have) cash, they _____ (use) credit.

They _____ (have) a good credit rating. They _____ (use) their department store credit cards, oil company credit cards, and other credit cards. They

_____ (use) the stores' credit plans to buy appliances and furniture. They

_____ (sign) credit contracts without reading them. Then the bills

_____ (begin) to come, and they _____ (keep) coming and coming.

Finally, Fred _____ (go) to a finance company to get one big loan to pay all his other loans. But Fred and his wife _____ (keep) buying things.

Fred _____ (decide) to get another job at night to pay the bills. But he

_____ (fall) asleep during the day because he _____ (work) all night at his other job. So his boss _____ (fire) him. Fred

_____ (not know) what to do. He _____ (begin) to rob banks.

But Fred _____ (not be) a very good bank robber. In a very short time the police _____ (catch) him.

When Fred _____ (get) out of jail, he and his wife _____ (promise) not to use credit again for five years. Fred and his wife have to break their habit.

They want a TV, but they now know that they must _____ (save) their money and buy things only when they can _____ (afford) them. They must

_____ (learn) to use credit wisely.

C. Answer the questions about Ken's life.

1948	**1953-1974**	**1974**	**1977**
born in New York	student in New York	became an architect	got married, moved to Pittsburgh

1. When did Ken live in New York?

2. What did he do in New York?

3. How long has Ken been an architect?

4. How long has Ken been married?

5. How long has he lived in Pittsburgh?

D. This is a résumé of Lisa's life. Imagine you are a reporter. Interview Lisa. Ask her questions about her life. Ask her questions about her future.

1949	**1951**	**1964-1967**
born in Ohio	family moved to Illinois	went to North High School

1967-1971	**1971**	**1972-1977**
attended the University of Chicago	traveled in Europe for six months	attended a university in New York

1977	**1977-present**	
got married and moved to Pittsburgh	professor at a university in Pittsburgh	

E. Rewrite this story in the past tense. Change *Barbara* to *Cindy and Ron.* Change the sentence *Now she's at the store* to *Yesterday they went to the store.*

Barbara has called many stores and gone to many stores to look for a TV. She has compared the stores' prices, services, and credit plans. She has finally decided which TV she wants to buy and where she wants to buy it. Now she's at the store. She is discussing the credit plan with the salesperson. They are looking at the credit contract. The credit contract lists the finance charge and the annual percentage rate (APR) of interest. The finance charge includes the interest and all the other fees for using credit. The interest (APR) in Barbara's credit contract is 18%. Barbara's reading the contract carefully. She's asking a lot of questions about the "fine print." She wants to make sure that she understands the contract. She wants to make sure that she knows exactly how much money she has to pay back. Before she signs the contract, she's going to make sure that there are no blank spaces.

Barbara's going to give the store a cash down payment. When she signs the contract, she's going to promise to pay the rest of the costs of the TV, the interest, and the finance charge in equal monthly payments (the installment plan).

F. Fill in the blanks to complete the dialogues.

Example: Ken: Where *have you been* all morning?

Lisa: I went to some garage sales.

Ken: Oh, no! *What did you buy?*

Lisa: I don't know what it is, but isn't it pretty!

Ken: Lisa, you complain about the way I shop at supermarkets. Look how you waste money at garage sales!

1.

Lisa: Where _____ since 10:00 a.m.?

Ken: I went to a few secondhand stores.

Lisa: _____?

Ken: To look for a washing machine.

Lisa: _____ a new one.

Ken: Used machines are cheaper.

Lisa: But Ken, you don't know anything about washing machines!

Ken: _____.

NOTE: Secondhand stores and garage sales are good places to buy used things at low prices. Sometimes you can save a lot of money. But you should know what to look for. If you buy a used washing machine at a garage sale, it won't have a warranty. If something goes wrong with it, you can't return it.

2.

Ken: Where _____ this morning?

Lisa: I was at the library.

Ken: _____?

Lisa: I was reading *Consumer Reports* about washing machines and dryers. It has a lot of information. You should read it, Ken.

3.

Ron: _____?

Cindy: I'm calling the Better Business Bureau.

Ron: _____?

Cindy: I want some information about the store we went to yesterday.

Ron: _____.

Cindy: I want to know if there have been any complaints against the store.

4.

Lisa: _____?

Ken: I'm looking in the Yellow Pages for names of stores that sell appliances. I'm going to call them to compare prices.

Lisa: _____?

Ken: Yes, I have. I checked the newspaper this morning for stores that have washing machines on sale.

NOTE: To save time and gas, use your telephone to compare prices and services. You can find the names and locations of furniture and appliance stores in the Yellow Pages of the telephone book. The Yellow Pages lists almost every business in your city. You can also check the newspapers. The newspapers have ads for stores that have appliances and furniture for sale. Often, the ads give the manufacturer's name, the model number, the price of the item, and sometimes the special features.

Before you call a store, you should know the name of the item, the manufacturer, the model number, and the color and size that you want.

5.

Ron: _____ an hour ago? I was looking for you.

Cindy: _____.

6.

_____ ever _____?

No, _____.

7.   How long _____?

_____ since 4:00!

8.   _____ tomorrow?

No, I can't. _____.

9.
Michael: Would you like to go to the movies tonight?

Barbara: _____.

Michael: How about Saturday night?

Barbara: _____.

10.
Barbara: Michael, I had a wonderful time Saturday night.

Michael: _____.

Reading

The Consumer Education class made this list of the steps for buying furniture and appliances.

1. Decide how much you can or want to spend on the furniture or appliance.

2. Plan before you shop.
   - Find out if you have a gas or electric connection in your house for the appliance.
   - Measure the space available for the appliance or furniture. Don't buy a sofa that fits in your living room but doesn't fit through your front door.

3. Learn everything you can about the product.
   - Ask your family and friends if they can recommend a brand or model.
   - Check *Consumer Reports* and other consumer guides. These are available in the library. *Consumer Reports* compares products and describes their advantages and disadvantages based on tests.
   - Decide what features you want. For example, do you really need all the extras on the deluxe model washing machine?
   - Compare operation and service costs of different brands and models.
   - Talk to salespeople. Ask questions about the safety and durability (how long it will last) of the product.
   - Read the labels. Look for appliances that meet the National Standard for Safety. Look for these seals: UL on electrical appliances and AGA on gas appliances. They mean that the product is safe. Furniture should have a tag that states the contents.

- Compare warranties (or guarantees). A warranty tells what the manufacturer or seller will do if something goes wrong with the product within a certain amount of time.
- Read the instructions in the operating manual.

4. Compare prices and services.
    - Ask your family and friends if they can recommend a store.
    - Check the prices at several stores. Look for sales. Remember, a higher price doesn't always mean better quality.
    - Compare the services at several stores:
        delivery
        installation
        repair service
    - Find out if delivery and installation are included in the price.
    - Only deal with reputable stores. You can call the Better Business Bureau to check on a store.

Comprehension Questions

Write the answers to the following questions.

1. What's the first step for buying furniture or appliances?

2. Before you buy furniture or an appliance, why should you measure your door at home?

3. What should you ask your family and friends?

4. What's *Consumer Reports?* Where can you find it?

5. Why should you compare operation costs of different brands and models?

6. What should you ask salespeople?

7. What seals can you find on appliances? What do they mean?

8. What's a warranty?

9. Does a higher price always mean that the appliance or furniture is better?

10. What services are available at some stores?

11. What's the Better Business Bureau? Why should you call it?

Listening Comprehension

Listen to the following conversations. Answer the questions based on the information in the conversation.

A. Ron's in a furniture store. He's looking for a sofa. He's talking to the salesperson.

1. How much is the sofa that the store advertised in the newspaper?

2. What's wrong with it?

3. How much is the other sofa?

4. Should Ron buy a sofa from this store?

B. Ken's in an appliance store looking for a washing machine. He's talking to the salesperson.

1. How much is the washing machine?

2. How long will it be on sale?

3. Does Ken need all the special features?

4. What will happen to the price of the washing machine tomorrow?

5. Should Ken buy this washing machine?

C. Cindy's in a store looking for a sofa. She's talking to the salesperson.

1. How much is the sofa?

2. How much is the down payment?

   3. How much is the weekly payment?

   4. How long do you make the weekly payments?

   5. Should Cindy buy a sofa from this store?

D. Barbara is in a store looking for a TV. She's talking to the salesperson.

   1. How much is the TV?

   2. Why does the salesperson say that Barbara should buy the TV now?

   3. Should Barbara buy a TV from this store?

E. Barbara's at a store looking for a TV. She's talking to the salesperson.

   1. How much was the TV that the store advertised in the newspaper?

   2. When did the store advertise the TV?

   3. Can Barbara buy it? Why?

   4. How much is the TV?

   5. Should Barbara buy a TV from this store?